JUMPSTART
your
CUSTOMER
SERVICE

JUMPSTART *your* CUSTOMER SERVICE

—10 JOLTS—

TO BOOST YOUR
CUSTOMER SERVICE

SHAWN DOYLE CSP
AND
LAUREN ANDERSON

Sound Wisdom

P.O. Box 310

Shippensburg, PA 17257-0310

Previously published as MO!: Live with Momentum, Motivation, and Moxie by Sound Wisdom

Previous ISBN: 1937879038

For more information on foreign distribution, call 717-530-2122.

Reach us on the Internet: www.soundwisdom.com.

ISBN 13 TP: 978-1-937879-41-9

ISBN 13 Ebook: 978-1-937879-42-6

For Worldwide Distribution, Printed in the U.S.A.

2 3 4 5 6 7 8 / 18 17 16 15 14

CONTENTS

Introduction 7

CHAPTER 1
The Chiliman: Hot Dog Hero 15

CHAPTER 2
Verne Oscarson: Fish Peddler Extraordinaire 25

CHAPTER 3
Liz Trotter: The American Maid Champion 37

CHAPTER 4
Carlos Nunez: JM Lexus One-of-a-Kind Service Advisor 47

CHAPTER 5
Bill Staton: The Amazing Maintenance Man 57

CHAPTER 6
Kate Holgate: The People Magnet 67

CHAPTER 7
Nicolas Rodrigues: Driving America 79

CHAPTER 8
Joe Fleming: Skycap with True Spirit. 91

CHAPTER 9
Pearl Deery: Pearls of Wisdom. 99

CHAPTER 10
Goldie Brown: Slipcover Maven 107

CHAPTER 11
Beatriz Farland: Be Inspired, Be Giving, Be Positive 117

CHAPTER 12
Customer Service Thoughts 127

INTRODUCTION

HELLO! Welcome to *Jumpstart Your Customer Service!* I am Shawn Doyle (waving to you on the right) and this is Lauren Anderson (she is waving elegantly on the left). Thanks for joining us. We are both professional speakers, trainers, and consultants. We have been doing what we do for over sixty years combined, and we have learned some valuable lessons during that time. We have both met and trained, coached, developed, and mentored thousands and thousands of people in different parts of the world throughout our careers as corporate employees and entrepreneurs who own our own respective companies. Over those years, we have noticed something independently and then together, and that is how the story of *Jumpstart Your Customer Service!* begins.

HOW JUMPSTART WAS BORN

It all started in a delivery room in Tampa, Florida, when the OB/GYN announced, "Congratulations, you have a baby. Jumpstart!" No, not really—we are just kidding. It started in a pub in

England when someone said "Get 'em. I know, I know, let's get some cables and jumpstart them!" No, that's not right either.

It actually started as a conversation Lauren and I were having one day. She was telling me about this amazing man who was a service advisor at an automobile dealership. As she excitedly told me his story, I was blown away. I said, "So let me get this straight: customers actually *call* to see if he is there at the dealership, and if he isn't they wait to bring their car in to be serviced?" She said yes. Then she told me they actually come to the dealership and take him out to lunch! As my British friends would say, I was *gobsmacked*! How could this be?

I then said to her, "That reminds me of a taxi driver I met in Washington, D.C., who wore a suit, tie, and hat and whose taxi was so immaculate you can eat off the floor." She said, "You mean a limousine?" I said, "No, a taxi." I also told her that he was the official taxi for many congressmen and senators who preferred him to a limo and also, by the way, paid him limo rates. Lauren could not believe it. So as we continued to bring up our various stories and examples, we came to a realization. It was like a bolt of lightning hit us, a true defining moment. These people had something! They all had a certain *je ne sais quoi*, an indescribable beautiful, magical quality about them.

These were people in ordinary jobs—or maybe different jobs that weren't so ordinary—but despite life experiences and adversity, they decided not to be ordinary. They performed their jobs brilliantly, exceptionally, differently, and exceeded everyone's expectations every day of what that job "should" be. More importantly, everyone around them knows it, sees it, and acknowledges it. We see it in the special people we meet as we travel, and in the people we meet in the classroom and after keynote speeches. They stand out. They shine. It was driving us crazy. What was *this quality*? We finally figured it out, nailed it down, and gave it a name—Jumpstart!

SO WHAT IS JUMPSTART?

Jumpstart is many things, but people who Jumpstart their customer service have defined qualities about them:

- Momentum: these people are a force who creates energy and momentum to make things go forward; but more than that, they *are* momentum.

- Motivated: these people are massively self-motivated and they even motivate others around them through the power of their special spark. It is absolutely contagious.

- Most extraordinary: you would never accuse these people of ever being ordinary, despite the fact they are in what some people would say are ordinary or mundane jobs. Not to them, they're not!

- Moxie: they have the courage, the ambition, and the initiative to take their job and turn it into something different. No run-of-the-mill service here. No one told them to, they just did.

- Monumental: their qualities are so special and monumental they become monuments or landmarks, an attraction unto themselves, a model of customer service (sometimes even over and above the business itself).

- Motion: they are always moving, innovating, and finding new ways to create and innovate in their jobs to improve their customer experience. They are never satisfied with the same old way. Ever.

- More: they do more, get more, make more, sell more, and have more satisfied customers who keep coming back for more.

- Mojo: some magical, mystical quality that makes them charm almost every person they meet. They could charm the rattles off a snake.

So here is our official definition of *Jumpstart Your Customer Service*:

customer service (noun or adjective): 1. people in ordinary jobs who perform at extraordinary levels with motivation, momentum, and moxie. 2. a special unique quality that makes people stand out and become a force of excitement and energy. 3. a difference maker in terms of customer service. 4. people who are in ordinary jobs but still have *it* (you know it when you see it; you can also feel it).

WHY YOU NEED A JUMPSTART!

Simply put, this modest little book could transform your customer service if you let it. Why? Because once you have it and apply it, you will have more money, more sales, and more customer satisfaction. Seriously, people are attracted and magnetized to people with the right customer service attitude like moths to an energy saver yellow light bulb. Aren't you? Aren't you attracted to people with passion and energy? Don't deny it—the chip in this book has a GPS and we will track you down! You know it is the truth. We are willing to help you get it. You know you want it, you need it, and you have it inside of you somewhere. Your organization needs it too. We are going to help you *Jumpstart Your Customer Service!*

HOW DO YOU GET THIS QUALITY?

You may have a Jumpstart attitude, or someone you know may have it. We assume that if you already have it, you want more of it (don't you?). If you don't have it, we're pretty positive you want it. So how do you get it? Well, as the world's only Jumpstart speakers (for now), we know the secrets and are willing to share them. We interviewed each of the special people in this book who have it and we were very inspired by them. We have been able to determine the special 4–8 qualities each of these special people have, and we have been able to boil down the essence of each of our subjects.

Here is the exciting part: we are going to provide the secrets to their special qualities and give you tips and techniques so that you can learn to *Jumpstart Your Customer Service!*

Can it be learned? Yes, we think so. Sure, some people are just naturals and have a high level of it already. But we think they are the exceptions and not the rule. Many of us didn't start out that way; we had people who inspired and taught us along the way in life and then one day, *blam!* we had it. We believe if you teach someone the attributes of people who have Jumpstart and let them work on it, combined with the right environment, you will have something special and great customer service skills will be learned. Think about it. We are the only species (as far as we know) who have the ability to change our lives through conscious thought, should we decide to. We don't think you would be reading this book if you weren't ready. So are you really, really, totally ready? Are your customer's waiting for this? Is your organization in need of it? Is your organization ready for it?

HOW THIS BOOK WORKS

Shawn was teaching a class at a bank in Charlotte, North Carolina, talking about motivation, passion, and an example of great, effective, unending, passionate customer service. He went to make a point about passion. In a spontaneous improvisational moment he said, "Passion is like...well, like Chiliman!" The class roared. All twenty-five people knew Chiliman by name! Chiliman, by the way, is Victor Werney, the guy who serves hot dogs outside of the building one day a week (on Thursdays). (We share his story in Chapter 1.) Shawn had watched him in action the week before. Why would they remember him? He doesn't even work for the bank. Why? He has *it*—that quality.

In this book you will read inspiring profiles of service advisors, hot dog vendors, seafood market owners, fitness trainers, taxi drivers, bakers and candlestick makers who all have the magic qualities. They are all normal people who work hard every day, but their work isn't normal. They love what they do. They do it in a passionate way that focuses on their customer, giving great customer service every time with every single person, day after day after day.

At the end of each profile you will see a summation of the 4–8 special qualities they have and our suggestions on how to incorporate them into your life and organization. This is how you can *Jumpstart Your Customer Service!*

We see people who are getting tired of media stars who are rich, privileged, had a silver spoon fed to them, and may even be famous for being famous or just stupidly lucky. We want to make our subjects the stars of this book. They have worked hard and made their own luck. As you will see, they were never handed anything except an opportunity and sometimes a paycheck. We believe they are the real heroes. And because they have done it, it might be easier to believe that you and your team can do it as well. Our goal is to make a difference in the world, and we think by sharing these stories, you can change it too.

One quick note about how to use this book: You will see at the end of each chapter two segments: Notes and WorkIT! Each of these segments has a very specific purpose. Notes are designed to summarize some of the key learning points from that particular person's life. In the WorkIT! segments you will find several suggestions on how to specifically apply these to your own life and work. All of these suggestions are either observable and measurable or tangible. That way they are not just vague ideas or concepts, but techniques that can be applied to your life now. *Comprende*, my friends?

So let's get moving. Here is our first story.

CHAPTER 1

THE CHILIMAN:
HOT DOG HERO

WHEN we first saw the Chiliman in Charlotte, North Carolina, we were amazed. Chiliman was outside of a bank building on a Thursday and had a long line of people who were patiently waiting to be served. While people were waiting in line, Chiliman kept up a constant patter of comedic lines; people in line were laughing and joking. He would ask them if they would like his own brand of Fluffy Bunny mustard on their hot dogs, or his world-famous custom Merlot-BBQ sauce (made with wine). Those in line could read various humorous signs when waiting: "Chili dogs making smarter-er. —Albert Einstein", and "If you lined up all the hot dogs we have ever served, it would really go a long way." Another sign read, "I am the only son of an only son of an only son."

When you think about it, this was extraordinary. Hot dog vendors are supposed to serve food, they're not supposed be a source of entertainment and a boost for morale. They are usually boring and not memorable in any way. They are not

15

supposed to be great at customer service. But that is not and never has been Victor Wernay's way of doing things. "It was never about hot dogs," he says. "It was always about becoming a legend." He says this in a way that is remarkable because it sounds like a passionate mission and not a statement of ego.

Victor started his career working in and around food service for various restaurants and food service businesses, like pizza places and coffee shops. He once worked as a manager of a pizza parlor and realized that most of all he really loved interacting and serving people. Customer service was at the core of his being.

At the pizza parlor where he was a manager, he created a very unique approach to serving pizza and interacting with customers. Each time a child came in with their family, they would color a picture, write their name on it, and then it was posted somewhere on walls of the restaurant. Eventually the entire interior of the restaurant was covered with children's drawings and colored pictures. This led to an interesting phenomenon; children would bring their families in to show off their work, which led to a significant increase in the business of the pizza parlor. It was a very popular and unique feature. Unfortunately, management decided that it was "too much" and took all the pictures down, leading to a significant dip in business.

At a coffee shop where Victor worked, he loved interacting and joking around with customers and was always able to put a smile on their face. But he soon grew weary of the coffee shop manager's approach. The manager criticized him for having coffee stains on the counter. Victor said, "Well, of course there's coffee stains on the counter; it's a coffee place!" The behaviors and the mindset of the corporate world and their bottom-line driven obsession "over the interest of people" was driving Victor crazy. They didn't care about customers the way he did.

Victor and his wife decided to take a vacation and travel around Europe for a while. They both had a lot of time to think. When they were driving around in the car one day, he asked his wife, "What do you think I should do?" She paused briefly and then said, "I think you should own a hot dog cart," and smiled. Victor thought that she was joking at first, and asked her if it was so. She said, "No, I think you have all the skills and abilities to own a hot dog cart. With your background and experience in food service, you have the personality to make it successful."

He thought about the concept for several weeks and asked friends about it, because for some reason it seemed to him like a silly idea. All of his friends were supportive and thought that he should go for it. He researched the cost of buying a hot dog cart and the licensing required and, as Victor says, "Sometimes you have a combination of good timing and luck." As luck would have it, a hot dog guy in downtown Charlotte at a popular corner happened to quit and that space was now available two days a week. The rest as they say, is history.

The former comedian and actor set up a hot dog stand at the corner of Fourth and Tryon in downtown Charlotte, North Carolina. "People have a choice when they get up every day," he said. "They can have a bad day or a good day. I choose good." He started talking up the crowds that lined up, joking with them, and had a new crazy saying on his sign every day. "I try to make a personal connection with each person. I think people really crave connection; it's a human need. I try to make a personal connection on some fact with each person. It might be about the weather, their name, the sports news of the day, whatever." He smiles and says, "Any boob with four thousand dollars can be a hot dog guy—but I want to be *the* hot dog guy—Chiliman!"

"One other lesson I learned early," says Victor, "is if people are slightly happy and not thinking about their wait in line, they don't mind it. Second (I learned this in the restaurant business), the people in the back of the line need to be acknowledged. As long as they are, they will stay too."

The business began to build and without actually seeking locations, he landed two days a week outside the bank offices and an additional day outside a law school. People were amused by his unique sauce names. "I notice things," says Chiliman, "and I thought the sauce names you see in stores for BBQ, and especially hot sauces, are awful and scary. You know, names like Hot Sauce Suicide or something like Skull Splitting Sauce with an evil looking skull on it. Who wants to eat that? So I have come up with names that sound better and more edible and nice, like Fluffy Bunny (mustard) and Fluffier Bunny (spicier mustard) and Cuddly Baby BBQ (mild) sauce and God's Gift to BBQ (you have to taste it)."

Why use such crazy product names? Victor says, "I am not really totally sure why, but I have always had a kind of obsession with naming things. When I was acting I had a card that said, 'Victor Wernay: actor, comedian, and legendary model for the visually impaired.'" He chuckles. "I know it's not politically correct, but they still remember the card. My goal is simple: one, to make people laugh, and two, to be remembered—not just for the product but also remembered as me." He has one hot sauce, one ketchup, five mustards, six mayonnaises, and five BBQ sauces. "I just love playing around with the food."

Victor's early years were shaped by a father who had a dry wit and a mother who was extremely extroverted. She acted in plays and would play the accordion for anyone who would listen. "No one wanted to hear the accordion," he reminded me. "No one ever does!" His Aunt Jeanetta was the "loose cannon" of the family; her loony humor at family get-togethers kept them all laughing and perhaps also shaped his own brand of humor today. He was also influenced by a drama teacher in high school, Art Gage. Art taught drama but most importantly encouraged Victor to get involved in Project Adventure, an Outward Bound style program. This built his confidence.

Chiliman thinks his keys to success and customer service are deceptively simple but hard to learn. "Always go for the personal connection. I go into Sam's Club Store to buy supplies and everybody who works there knows me, is glad to see me, and greets me. I gotta tell ya, it blows my friends' minds. I may take it to the extreme, but people love to be connected with—everyone."

One hot day a man came up to his cart with a dog and ordered a hot dog, a soda, and a bottle of water. Chiliman handed him the hot dog, soda, the bottle of water, and a cup. The man looked at the cup and asked, "What is the cup for?" Victor smiled and said, "The cup is for your dog. I know the soda is for you but the water is for your dog." The man was amazed, but Victor says, "That is the extra touch, the extra mile. That is service, the little details." The service is so great that he averages about 15 percent in tips each day in addition to the regular revenue. No one tips hot dog guys, right?

Chiliman has customers that are so loyal they walk by his cart and say in a guilty tone, "I am sorry, I can't buy your food today. I have to go to a business luncheon." The bond that has been created makes them feel obligated to stop and buy from him.

Victor says, "The irony is that I have never chased anything. I am doing what I do and it just happens. New locations get offered; people ask me to set up at festivals. It just happens that way." He is currently working on a possible deal to package and distribute his sauces. "They met me and asked me...like I said, it just happens." We leave Chiliman wearing a crazy hat and joking with a woman about her name. She is laughing and smiling while she buys a hot dog.

NOTES

1. **Connection.** Go out of your way to find some method or technique to connect with people. In an age of technology and impersonal connections, people want to be connected with in a personal and individual way. As Chiliman says, "They crave it."

2. **Be original.** The signs with the funny sayings, the humor, the original sauce names—they are all original and, more importantly, memorable. We simply forget the average but remember the extraordinary and unique. We also tell our friends about it, creating buzz and word of mouth advertising (which is the best kind).

3. **Serve people.** When you serve people and don't worry about rules and regulations and things being too much, they respond. Well-meaning managers eliminate things people like for their own business reasons, but they are not the reasons of the customers. The consequence is angry customers, and lost business and sales.

4. **Reinvent your category.** There were plenty of hot dog stands before Chiliman, but by using unique approaches and ideas, he changed his category. He has no competition. People want to wait in line for the food and the show.

5. **Be observant.** Look around at the world, the business, and your customers. Think about what they want. Watch what they do. Look at products and try to make them better. Look at every detail. Look at the product names, packaging, and how they are sold. Keep your eyes open to possible opportunity.

WorkIT!

Think about your business or your role at the business you work for. Make a list of things that your customers respond to positively. Try to make changes that are in accordance with that list.

_____

_____

_____

_____

_____

_____

Pull out a piece of paper. On that paper, write down a list of at least five ways you can connect better with your customers. It might be on social media, such as Twitter or LinkedIn, or it may be ways in which you can connect better in person.

_____

_____

_____

_____

_____

_____

How can you be more unique in your products and services offered? Sit down with a group of coworkers and brainstorm a list of ways you can be unique and different from your competition.

_____

_____

_____

_____

_____

Take some quiet time alone to think through what you're currently doing for a living. Do you have a passion for it? If you don't, figure out a plan to get out of that industry in the next year and do what you have a passion for.

_____

_____

_____

_____

_____

_____

CHAPTER 2

VERNE OSCARSON:
FISH PEDDLER EXTRAORDINAIRE

IN any coastal area, there are a lot of places to buy fish. A ton of them, in fact. So it's no surprise that south Florida is the same. In the Fort Lauderdale/Miami region, fishing is a huge industry. There are thousands of professionals and amateurs catching and selling fish and other seafood. Most fish markets are all the same, at least to the untrained eye. However, even with all the places to shop, there are many customers who only go to one place to buy seafood and won't take their business anywhere else. That place is Fish Peddler East, located in Fort Lauderdale, Florida.

Why? Aren't they all the same? What is this place's secret weapon? Simply put, it is Verne Oscarson, his wonderful employees, and his great customer service. If you speak to the store's owner, Verne Oscarson, you would know right away he is the Fish Peddler East, for his passion, drive, and charisma are magnetic. He is passionate about fish, what he does, and, most importantly, about his customers.

Verne has a passion for the business and making people feel good about what they are purchasing. It's evident in the way he speaks about his trade. He has a twinkle in his eye. You can also tell by how amazingly neat and clean he keeps his market. It's visible in how carefully he prepares the fish, like a work of art. Most of all, it is obvious that Verne loves what he does when you learn about how hard he's worked to get to where he is today. He earned it. There was no silver spoon in this man's mouth.

Originally from Wisconsin, Verne's family moved to Fort Lauderdale in 1969. As luck would have it, his school, Fort Lauderdale High School, just happened to be across the street from a restaurant, the Sea Grille. He started working there part-time, and before he knew it, he ended up in the kitchen. "I think I started peeling shrimp," he recalls, smiling. The longer he worked there, the more he learned about the business.

Verne enrolled in college, and met his future wife two years later. As he puts it, "College went to the wayside, and we started building a life." Seafood was what he knew, so he continued to learn more about it while gaining work experience, so much so that he became the assistant kitchen manager of the Sea Grille.

During his eight years in the restaurant business, he met various sellers who supplied the fish to the restaurants. He didn't know it at the time, but he was building his knowledge for the future. One of these sellers was a man named Paul Smith, who owned a market called Pop's Fish Market in Deerfield Beach. Verne began working at the fish market part-time, and it eventually became his full-time job.

Still in the seafood business, the retail seafood and restaurant seafood industries were quite different, as Verne had been learning. He was amazed by the differences and the subtleties involved. He explains, "Now, you're not cooking your seafood dinner for somebody, you're supplying them with the raw materials for them to cook their own dinners. Being in the restaurant side of the business, you were familiar with purveyors of already-processed products that come through the back door. And then when you get into a retail fish market, which is dealing with the boats, the direct source, it's a completely different animal. Another major element is dealing with customers." Soon Verne was head over heels in love (or maybe fin over tails) with the fish market business.

One day, Verne visited a store called the Fish Peddler, which he found to be very impressive. The products were of high quality, the absolute best that could be sold. Customer service was of utmost importance; if a customer needed anything, the Fish Peddler's employees would do whatever they could to provide it to them. They treated customers like friends and family, not merely like ordinary customers as in so many other businesses. Customer service ruled.

Verne also liked the feel of the store, which had a "comfortable, friendly, almost seaside atmosphere to shop in." He began working at the Fish Peddler, originally being hired as the assistant to the general manager. He later became the general manager, and when the Fish Peddler's owners retired, he found investors and bought the business in 1996. That is when he was able to put his personal stamp on the market, keeping all the positives and making it even better.

So why won't customers buy their seafood anywhere else? Of course, the quality of the food is one of the reasons. The biggest reason, however, is the people who work there and the relationships they have with their customers. Verne trains every employee to be in tune with the customer and what they want, to remember them when they return, and to acknowledge that. He also strives to not only sell seafood but also to educate his customers about their food and give them suggestions on how to prepare it. Would this ever happen in the fish department at a giant grocery store? Rarely. Grocery store employees don't have the time, they wouldn't expend the extra energy it takes, and all too often they do not have the knowledge.

People also like to shop at Verne's store because they become familiar and comfortable with each of the employees. Because they're happy working there, employees stay at Fish Peddler East for a long time. In a world of "big box" stores, Verne has built a small, warm neighborhood market. It's the kind we all miss from our childhood, where everybody knew everyone by name, and where we were all connected somehow.

Verne's employees love him and love working for him. Anyone would be fortunate to work for someone like Verne. He has learned, through previous employers, how to (and how not to) treat the people he hires. He believes a positive attitude yields positive results, and people should be compensated for their work. "If someone is capable of doing a job," he explains, "they should be paid well for doing that job, and they'll flourish." This is an interesting concept in the fast food, minimum wage marketplace (we like to call this internal customer service).

Verne likes to hire people and personally trains them—especially kids, to "give them a chance"—in all aspects of the business. There is no specialization at Fish Peddler East. Verne wants them to understand the business inside and out, the way he learned it. So how does he know whom to promote? His answer is remarkably simple yet very wise. "If somebody does a spectacular job washing dishes," he explains, "chances are, they'll do a spectacular job at the next level up."

He also possesses what is an unusual quality these days: loyalty. The general manager that he worked with at the Fish Peddler is now the general manager at Fish Peddler East. And the man who hired Verne at the Sea Grille when he was seventeen now works for Verne as well. Huh? So the employee is now the boss, and the boss is the employee. That is called loyalty.

The kids these days call something from the past "old school," and this can be an insult or a criticism. But in Verne's case no one would ever use that as a criticism. They would say that old-fashioned values like hard work, commitment to customers, giving great customer service, and paying people well for their hard work are novel ideas. In the age of fast food and low pay, poor customer service and lack of loyalty on both the part of employers and employees, maybe—just maybe—Verne has something special. Maybe by looking back we can look forward to some new models of how to thrive in business, keep great employees, and lifelong customers.

As we walk away from the market, Verne is educating a customer on exactly the best way to fix and prepare a lovely, bright red snapper. I get the distinct feeling this is something he will never retire from. I myself have often prepared my seafood purchased at the Fish Peddler East exactly the way Verne taught me too. And I don't regret it.

NOTES

1. **Customer service rules.** Internal service to your employees and outstanding service to your customers will set you apart and inspire folks. People will talk about you and your company, often sending more customers to you.

2. **Be loyal.** Verne is so loyal that he hires people who used to hire him. In today's world where we lack connection and stability, loyalty can go a long way. So how can you follow his lead and be more loyal to your professional contacts, your family, and your friends?

3. **Be passionate.** No matter what business you are in, be passionate about it. Yes, people could thumb their nose and say, "Eww—fish?" but what about being the best? What about being world class? How can your passion make a difference for you as an employee? With Verne, it gets you promoted. The same applies everywhere else too. How can passion make a difference if you are a leader? How can it make a difference if you own a business?

4. **Train them.** Training people—what a concept! You mean they shouldn't just figure it out on their own? In Verne's own words, "Give people a chance," and train them in all aspects of the business. Teach them what you expect of them;

show them how and they will succeed. Make customer service paramount in the training process and your employees will reward you tenfold with repeat customers over and over again. We have been in the training and development industry a long time. We have seen with our own eyes the remarkable difference it makes when people get development and when they are taught how to do what is expected of them. What can you do to train someone around you?

5. **Learn the business.** You saw that Verne spent many years learning about seafood in both the retail and restaurant arenas. At some point, he became an expert. Strive to learn everything about your business and your customers. Read, study, follow the trade magazines of your industry, and go to shows and events, know the demographics of your community and listen to what your customers are telling you they want. Apprentice, get mentored, get education and training, and gain experience. We see too many people who want to be vice president in a few short years without understanding the ins and outs of their respective business. Create an individual learning plan to learn your business and to really learn about your customer. Go out and talk to your customers, listening to what they are saying with your third ear (what they really mean by what they are saying).

WorkIT!

Do you ask customers what they think of your company and how it can be better?

_____

_____

_____

_____

_____

Do you regularly thank your customers for their business?

_____

_____

_____

_____

_____

Do your customers know they can give you their opinion and that you value it? How do you act on those opinions?

_____

_____

_____

_____

_____

When was the last time you picked up a book to learn about how to give better customer service? How about the people you work with?

_____

_____

_____

_____

_____

When was the last time you or the folks you work with went to a training session on customer service?

_____

_____

_____

_____

_____

When was the last time you had a company or department discussion on your level of customer service and how to improve it?

_____

_____

_____

_____

CHAPTER 3

LIZ TROTTER:
THE AMERICAN MAID CHAMPION

THE first thing that strikes you about Liz Trotter when you meet her is her huge white smile, her energetic eyes, her spiky hair, and the stylish glasses that look like something that an evening news anchor would wear—very smart. She smiles as if she is almost keeping a secret, and maybe she is. After all, she has one of the most successful cleaning companies in the Olympia, Washington, area. Few people would realize that she has built her cleaning company from nothing into a million-dollar business.

One could almost assume that she was born with a silver spoon in her mouth, but that would be the furthest thing from the truth...and a joke to Liz Trotter. Actually, Liz has experienced a great deal of adversity and tragedy in her life. The fact that she has been able to overcome all of that tragedy is a testament to her iron will and tenacity.

The lid of Liz Trotter's life when lifted reveals a very tough childhood, although Liz doesn't necessarily see it that way. For her it was just a stepping-stone to the life that she's created for herself today. When Liz was very young, her mom was struggling to afford to take care of her children, so she sent them away to an orphanage. Later on, around the age of nine, her father came and rescued them from the orphanage to go and live with her dad and her stepmom. While this sounds like a happy ending, it was actually the beginning of a long nightmare. Both parents worked full-time and the stepmom worked two jobs, which meant Liz, the oldest of eight kids, was responsible for watching her seven siblings. At the age of eleven she became the mother by default.

Her childhood is a series of scenes of both mental and physical abuse. Her father, being very abusive, would force the kids to get into the pool in the wintertime when the water was freezing cold to get the leaves off the bottom of the pool. He would then take the leaf skimming net on the end of the pole and hold their head under if they were not doing a good job in an attempt to punish them for their lack of work ethic. She was punched and kicked, slapped and yelled at, and was held responsible for any poor behavior of the other children. Her father often would have the kids run around the backyard while sadistically shooting them at close range with a pellet gun.

One of Liz's most unpleasant memories is of her father having all the kids line up, and kid number one would have to take a belt and whip kid number two, and so on. If it was not hard enough, kid number one would be punished. Liz never knew when it would be a good day or bad day at home. When you ask her how she was able to survive the abuse of the home that she lived in, she said she knew that "her dad did not hate her; it was just something wrong with him." Despite all of this, however, she graduated high school.

At the age of seventeen, it's no surprise that Liz decided to escape by moving out of the home and living with her boyfriend. Of course, when she moved she spent a lot of time worrying about the siblings she had left behind. She got pregnant at the tender age of seventeen and had a little girl. When her daughter had just begun to walk, Liz was driving her late model car on New Year's Eve while her brother was holding baby Kristin on his lap. Going through an intersection, Liz's car got T-boned by a drunk driver and Kristen was tragically killed.

Liz went through several years of pain and sorrow, but she continually stayed focused on her future—searching for her place in the world. She went to junior college for a little while. She then went to beauty school, dropped out without completing it, lived with a friend (sleeping on the couch), and was even homeless for a short time. She tried to go back to college again but was just having a hard time finding her passion.

At the age of twenty-two, Liz was married for the first time and moved to Washington State. There she had a new daughter, Shara, and the ultimate irony—she decided to start a day care in her home, watching eight children. As she looks back on it now, she knew nothing about the profession of childcare and didn't have any of the proper licenses or certifications to be a proper childcare facility, but somehow it fed her soul. After a time of healing with so many young children, she realized she needed a better job; she needed more out of her life.

One of the best turns of fortune for her was when she met a business owner, a Korean gentleman by the name of Jin Soo Na. He owned a series of Korean dry cleaners called South Sound Cleaners. Jin was nice to Liz. She worked very hard and always looked after the business. He became her valuable business mentor.

They were the perfect match. Liz was the young energetic person who worked hard and could understand Jin's heavy Korean accent. She helped him with whatever he wanted in terms of dealing with lawyers, contracts, setting up bank accounts, and making deposits. She always got results. A true entrepreneur at heart, Jin Soo Na decided to open a florist and asked Liz to run it. He always asked the same question, "How much money it cost? How much money we make? When?"

Liz was the perfect employee; results-oriented, committed, liked to work hard, and really did not care about the money. Her philosophy was always that she had enough to do what she needed to do. Coming from a background of scarcity and abuse, having enough was enough—she had learned about acceptance at a very early age. Around that time her marriage fell apart and she got divorced. She felt like she had learned as much from her business mentor as she could and was ready to strike out on her own.

When thinking about starting a new business, she thought, "Well, I know a lot about cleaning, being the eldest of eight children; and I know a lot about chemicals, having run a dry cleaner for multiple years; so why not start a cleaning service for cleaning residential homes and offices?" She had an "in" and she was ripe for the opportunity.

Liz has always been curious about learning new things. She never gave up and she's never stopped learning, always wanting to be prepared for what the future would bring. Seventeen years ago the company American Maid Cleaning was born. With her daughter, Shara, her new husband, Tim, and their newborn son, Gavin, working daily for 16–20 hour days, her company started to grow quickly and she started adding friends and more family to her staff. The company grew and has become very successful, with over twenty-seven employees.

What would really strike you as a customer is how very unique and different the American Maid Company is. They are obsessed with customer service. The people who clean the houses are crisply dressed in uniforms, but not the kind you would expect. They wear basketball uniforms with a beautiful red, white, and blue theme, and Crocs. Instead of each member of the team having a number on his or her jersey, they have a letter on it, and that's how you know the order they were hired in. So if you have someone come to your house and they have a C on their jersey, you will know that they were the third employee hired. And they're happy—they love their jobs.

While cleaning toilets might not make it high on their list of favorite things to do, working for American Maid is something they can feel proud of. It is quite a sight to see them pull up to a home and have five basketball team members jump out of their vehicle and race to clean the inside of the house, using a mix of sports terms to describe their business. For example, if a house is not cleaned well, a client complains, and they have to go back and re-clean it, that is known as a free throw. The employees are team members and they refer to their clients as fans. This, along with the fresh baked cookies they leave at each newly cleaned home, really gets people's attention—it's both original and different! Talk about service.

Liz has goals of expanding her maid service by perhaps franchising in the future with more locations, and is even thinking about coaching other cleaning companies on how to build their businesses. Most people would wonder, "Why is it that Liz was able to be successful despite her upbringing of physical and mental abuse?" When asked, she says, "It is actually fairly simple: I did not want to have that kind of life because it was icky."

She told me that she wanted to make sure that her children were not treated that way and that they would not have to grow up with the scars that she has from her upbringing. She was going to change the abuse cycle. Liz says, "I learned early on that my life could be exactly what I wanted it to be, and every day for me is a great day! After all, I was trained by life's experiences. If my car breaks down I think, 'Oh well, it could be worse—a *lot* worse.' With the life I have lived and experienced, I know what worse looks like!"

Remarried to a wonderful man for the past sixteen years has helped Liz create the peaceful life she craved in her youth. She lives her life today as she always has—as an optimist. She says to herself, "I'm looking forward to what is coming because something great is right on the horizon!" Looking at the future has always made any problems seem dim regardless of the circumstances surrounding her life.

Her employees are weirdly loyal to her. When asked why, she states very simply, "We just accept our people, and I think they can feel that." (Besides, who wouldn't want to wear cool uniforms like that?) She makes it a point to learn about her employees and to understand them, to treat them like a family and to help them feel accepted because many times they've never felt acceptance in their lives before.

When I asked her if there were any final words she would like to say, she said, "Well, this may sound odd, but I have always been lucky—just completely super lucky. Great things always happen to Liz Trotter." I couldn't have said it better myself. Liz Trotter is an amazing woman who emulates a customer service mindset.

NOTES

1. **Be curious.** Liz was always curious about learning the dry cleaning business, the florist business, and the home cleaning business. Do you maintain an amazing level of curiosity about learning and studying new things?

2. **People awareness.** Try as much as possible to understand why people do what they do and say what they say. It doesn't mean you have to agree with them, it's just important to genuinely try to understand them. That is, after all, what service is all about.

3. **It's okay to be afraid.** Liz actually used fear as a motivator to keep her moving forward. So if you are fearful, that's okay—just use that fear as energy to drive you forward.

4. **Be tolerant.** Liz is willing to be tolerant about how people are instead of trying to change them. She accepts them in their current state. Because she is willing to do this, she gets a different response from people rather than if she was judgmental.

5. **Be an optimist.** Many people say, "What is there to be optimistic about?" Liz reminds us not to get stuck in whatever plight we find ourselves in, but to "look forward to what is coming—something great is right on the horizon."

WorkIT!

Write down a list of "bad things" that have happened to you in the past as it relates to customer service, and how they've impacted you. Then, beside each of those items, write down how you *cannot* allow them to happen to your customers and how you're going to go about changing that.

_____

_____

_____

_____

_____

Create a personal learning plan. Many people tell us that their company does not have a training department for learning—so make your own. Sit down and decide the items you want to improve on. Create at least one learning action item for each one.

_____

_____

_____

_____

_____

_____

Try to learn more about human nature and psychology. Pick at least two to three books to read this year about human psychology or behavior. Books like *Emotional Intelligence* by Daniel Goleman or the *Platinum Rule* by Dr. Tony Alessandra are a couple of examples. Understanding more about human nature will help you get along with people more effectively and make you much better at customer service. What books will you read?

_____

_____

_____

_____

_____

Think about the types of people for which you have no tolerance, and try to figure out why you don't have tolerance for them. Come up with a plan to create more tolerance and understanding toward each of those folks. Pick one person per week to work with. Keep in mind that they will not know that you're doing this; they will just see you're being more tolerant with them. This will help you give better service to your internal team.

_____

_____

_____

_____

_____

CHAPTER 4

CARLOS NUNEZ:
JM LEXUS ONE-OF-A-KIND
SERVICE ADVISOR

GOING to your local car dealership for a car checkup or repair is usually like going to the dentist to have half of your teeth pulled, but not if you own a Lexus, live in south Florida, and are lucky enough to have Carlos Nunez as your service advisor. He is so popular, respected, trusted, and loved that many of his customers come in to try to take him to lunch or just hang out with him for a while, even when their car is not being serviced. What is this about? It is all about Carlos and his special customer relations.

As I was waiting to interview Carlos, there were five customers also waiting for him. I jokingly said, "It's like JFK Airport in a holding pattern: stacked up and trying to land." One of the customers heard me and replied, "If that were the case, Carlos would bring us a helicopter and we would land first." It is all about Carlos. It is obvious from the moment you see how he interacts with his customers that he is going to service them, and to his utmost. No questions asked. When you see the smiles and reactions of his customers, they believe he will take care of everything.

It is evident from the moment you meet Carlos that he is a passionate, energetic, knowledgeable guy. You feel it in his handshake, see it in his eyes and smile, and hear it in his words and tone—he loves and cares about what he does and cannot wait to help his customers through their service appointment or issue. You also get the feeling that Carlos would be great at anything he chose to do in life. He knows what people need, what they want, and he is there to do what he can to deliver that. He gets *it*.

Born in Brooklyn, New York, from Puerto Rican-born parents, Carlos, his sister, and his three brothers (one adopted) had to go to work at early ages. Their parents were factory workers earning $50 a month, so everyone had to help out to make ends meet. At eleven, Carlos was working unloading trucks to earn enough money to buy sneakers. He then worked cleaning a grocery store at night—washing the floor, stocking shelves, and setting up displays. He loved it and took great pride in it.

He learned from his father that "good things happen to people who work hard," and that lesson has stayed with him to this day. With five kids, and earning only $50 a month, his parents paid off their home in Brooklyn in just eleven years!

During summers, Carlos also worked for the local police in the community affairs department, taking poor, underprivileged kids on outings and vacations out of the city. He continued to work hard and started going to college. After five years,

Carlos graduated from Queens College, the first ever college graduate in his family.

After Carlos graduated, a friend moved to south Florida and suggested Carlos would love it too. So Carlos moved down there. Within ten days he had an apartment, a car, and a job working for Enterprise Rent-A-Car as a rental agent. (Now, that's a mover and a groover.) He learned he had a gift for talking to people, and he used his ability to develop business with local body shops and dealerships. He loved giving everyone he met the very best of himself.

He quickly became the manager at Enterprise. Carlos developed relationships with his customers, buying them donuts and coffee or lunch, and playing softball with them on the weekends. He liked to talk to people, make them feel good, and fix their problems. Eventually he was promoted to vice president and was moved back to New York.Missing his wife and two children who were six and seven years of age, however, Carlos left the position and eventually moved back to Florida. He landed a sales job for a construction company, where he once again used his skills and enthusiasm along with his ability to build strong relationships.

Carlos heard about a rental manager position for Toyota Rental Car Company based at JM Lexus through a friend. This was where Lexus customers would come to get a rental/loaner car while their car was being serviced. Having experience in this field, and loving customer service, Carlos interviewed for the job, landed it, was given a car, and doubled his previous salary. He started the very next day. Six months later, unfortunately, the rental car company took this location under their own ownership, and Carlos was out of a job.

JM Lexus saw and heard that Carlos Nunez had great relationships with the Lexus customers who were getting rental/loaner cars. He knew how to create relationships through great customer service, so they offered him a position at JM Lexus as a customer service adviser. He is still happily in this position today after eighteen years, even after being offered many opportunities to become a manager elsewhere.

Carlos knows people like to be around happy, upbeat, can-do people. He believes in helping his customers, giving them what they need, and doing it right. When asked what lessons he would teach young people going into business today, he says, "Treat people like you want to be treated: be honest, be ethical, look them in the eyes, and tell the truth. Think about the customer before yourself. Prioritize what the customer needs and the other stuff will come later. Be flexible and open to change, and do not let that affect your job."

When some coworkers were complaining one day after Hurricane Ike caused all the main Lexus computers to go down, causing lost communication and business, Carlos said, "We just have to work smarter and harder to make up what we lost. It could be worse: we could have worked at the Lexus dealership in Galveston, Texas, where the hurricane destroyed their homes, business, and everything."

Even with pay cuts in these hard economic times, Carlos has never earned less; he has just worked smarter and harder to make up for it. He follows the example of his immigrant parents: "Good things happen to people who work hard." He added his authentic, successful customer service attitude to all of life.

Carlos is a positive, high-energy person with great customer service. He does not take what he does for granted. Customers are *it* for him. They are what make him a success. He often tells his coworkers, "I am not here to be your friend, even though that would be nice. I am here to take care of my customers and to satisfy my bosses." He looks at his job as if he has five mortgages to pay: his own and those of the four technicians dependant on him to come to work every day. He considers them his internal customers. He has had only two sick days in fifteen years. He often visits his customers in the hospital and attends funerals. He really cares.

It is not uncommon for Carlos to have a line of fifteen customers after he goes on vacation for a few days, because his customers wait for him to return. He is a happy guy who loves his job, makes it fun, and at the same time takes what he does very seriously. Customer service is a passion of his, and, when you experience Carlos and see him in action, you want to do the same thing—you want to be like him. Good things really do happen to people who work hard and put the customer first in every instance.

NOTES

1. **Be passionate about all of it.** Be passionate about what you do and about how you do it. If you are going to do a job, do it with every ounce of passion and energy you can muster. Show others how much you love what you do. They will notice it. Customers want to go to someone who is passionate. Usually, passion and confidence translate as "competence" to a customer. In a retail store, for example, the person busy talking, selling, or just putting away stock is the one customers go to for answers to their questions—even if it just is, "Where is the restroom?" Passion is infectious; you can change the other folks you work with.

2. **Give respect.** Respect what you do, how you do it, and the people with whom you do it. Be respectful to others: coworkers, bosses, and customers. When you give respect and show that you respect others and your company by doing a great job, good relationships are built. Good relationships are lasting. The folks you have lasting relationships with will bring others to you.

3. **Work hard and smart.** Nothing in life comes easy. Work hard and smart at whatever you do. No matter how you look at it, it takes work— hard work and consistency in that hard work— as well as working smart, to make a difference

in your job. Carlos and his father are proof that good things do happen to people who work hard and smart.

4. **Relocate.** Sometimes you will need to relocate for a new opportunity. Being open to relocation is also a great message to employers that you are willing to do what it takes for the job. It also shows that you are flexible and a reasonable risk taker—which are both good qualities.

5. **Look at the big picture.** Like Carlos, think about the others you work with and how what you do affects them. Be conscious of how you may affect their performance, their workload, and how eventually they, in turn, may affect you. What you do can be infectious. If you are in a customer service business, be infectious. At work, talk about customer service and how to do it better. Try new techniques, discuss the results, have open dialog. This will help everyone get better. Eventually everyone will be giving great customer service as a natural habit. Try it and see your company shine.

WorkIT!

Do you have at least three favorite customer service techniques? Make a list of the techniques you use successfully, and purposefully use these with every customer.

_____

_____

_____

_____

_____

_____

Do you share your techniques with others you work with, and do they share theirs with you? If not, do so and discuss how to improve your customer service by using these successful techniques.

_____

_____

_____

_____

_____

_____

_____

_____

Do you have a customer service mentor? If not, get one. Discuss views on customer service.

_____

_____

_____

_____

_____

_____

How does your mentor's view on customer service differ from yours? List them below.

_____

_____

_____

_____

_____

What do you plan to do to improve your own customer service now that you have shared opinions on this with others?

_____

_____

_____

_____

_____

Do you show your passion at your job? List the ways in which you show your passion.

_____

_____

_____

_____

_____

_____

CHAPTER 5

BILL STATON:
THE AMAZING
MAINTENANCE MAN

I was staying at a hotel in Durham, North Carolina, when the air conditioner in my room started making a horrible racket. At around eight o'clock at night, I made the decision that I needed to call the front desk to get the air conditioner fixed; otherwise, I predicted I would have a long evening. I was so glad I called the front desk, as I was able to meet an amazing man named Bill Staton. There is no question that Bill possesses all the qualities needed to be great at customer service.

When Bill first came to my door and knocked, I opened the door and he said, "Good evening, sir." He was crisply dressed in his maintenance man uniform and was also wearing a big bright smile. As soon as he arrived in my room, I immediately knew I was talking to someone special. He treated me in a way that I can only describe as being an honored guest in someone's home. He carefully took the vent cover off of the air conditioning unit and shined his flashlight in to see what was causing the racket.

As he was doing his work, standing on a small stepladder, he engaged me in lively conversation. When he asked what I did for work, I told him that I was a professional speaker. "Wow," he said, "that is really something. That is something I have always been interested in myself." He then asked why I was in town, to whom I was speaking, and what my topic was the following day. He listened with a careful ear, not with an attempt to respond, taking it all in. He was long, lean, fit, and had beautiful walnut-colored skin. I knew he was older but he looked much younger. He had an energy about him.

"Well," he said, "I think I have this all figured out, and I know what is causing the problem. He tinkered around for a while, made some adjustments, and turned the air conditioner blower back on. It kicked on quietly, and he reached up and covered the vent with a piece of paper. "What is that for?" I asked curiously. He said, "Well, I can't have this air conditioner blowing oil all over your room, can I?" This was followed by a big smile. Once the air conditioner unit seemed to be behaving itself, he removed the paper and white particles flew out of the vent onto the carpet and on top of the dresser. He sighed, "Well, that won't do. I kind of had a feeling that was going to happen. I'll be right back if, you don't mind."

Once he left the room, I realized that the air conditioning system was purring like a quiet kitten. A few moments later there was a polite knock at my door. "Okay," Bill said. "Let's see if we can get you fixed up." In one hand he had a vacuum cleaner and in the other he had a soft rag and some cleaner. I watched him as he meticulously vacuumed every speck of foreign dust off of the carpet, and carefully wiped off the surface above my desk and dresser in my room.

"You don't really need to do all that," I said. He looked up and smiled, taking pride in his work. "You are a guest in our hotel. Here is the way I see it. Probably sometime later you're going to want to kick off your shoes and walk around the room. I don't want you to have to have white stuff all over your nice black socks." I thanked him for his extra effort.

He told me that the year before he had thirty-nine positive comment cards filled out about him. Keep in mind that he does not work at the front desk or in the restaurant, and he is not a bellman. He is simply a maintenance man. But he's actually much more than that: he's a maintenance man with a keen eye for detail and an amazing awareness about customer service. He treats people with respect.

"Thank you for fixing that, Bill. I am sure I will sleep better tonight. I noticed earlier you had mentioned an interest in public speaking. What did that mean, if I may ask?"

"Well," he said, "my life is quite a story, and it has been a lot of ups and downs. But I would like to share my story through speeches and books because I think it would help young people a lot." We sat and talked for over thirty minutes, like long-lost friends. His story was amazing.

Born in 1955, Bill grew up on the very rough and tough streets of Harlem, New York. It was a hardscrabble life and Bill's father was nowhere around; his mother, who dropped out of school in the eighth grade, was on public assistance and an alcoholic. At a very young age, Bill, being the oldest, became the guardian and protector of his two younger sisters, Lynetta and Lisa, and his brother, Eric. All the folks in the neighborhood started calling him "little man" because he was the one who had to take care of his family.

Although he is not proud to admit it, there were times in his teenage years when he had to steal or even sell marijuana in order to feed his family. For Bill it was always about the love of his family. "You know," Bill said philosophically, "sometimes I was so tired and worn-out I just had to leave it up to God. I thought that he would take care of us as I was always trying to do the right thing—taking care of my family. I am sometimes embarrassed about what I had to do, but I had to do it."

Despite all of his family's difficulties, Bill still managed to make time to play on his high school basketball team, dreaming of one day playing at the professional level. He knew he was going to go to college. He didn't know how he was going to make it happen because he did not have the money, but he just knew he would. Bill made it happen.

A former shop teacher from his high school, and who now worked at New England College, was able to get Bill a basketball scholarship. All he had to pay for was room and board and keep his marks up. It was a dream come true for a kid who had talent and motivation. Things went great in that first year, and Bill was really enjoying his college years. At the end of that year, however, a letter arrived from his mom. That letter changed the course of his life.

The letter outlined that his mom was struggling, his brothers and sisters were all staying in different places, they had no money left, and if he did not come back and take care of things, they were even going to cut off her welfare. Bill then decided that the family's guardian angel had to go back home, so he dropped out of school. He went back to work and landed a job at Montgomery Ward, where he worked very hard starting in the mailroom, was soon promoted to the advertising department, and even did occasional modeling. "I have always been a people person," Bill said, "and they can always tell."

During those years Bill married and started a family. He moved to Atlanta for fifteen years. After getting a divorce, he learned that his mother was sick battling Alzheimer's disease, so he moved to North Carolina to take care of her. The move from Georgia to Carolina and all the expenses of taking care of his mom used up all of Bill's savings. He knew he needed to get a job. Unfortunately, the area where his mom lived in Wilson, North Carolina, did not have much employment.

In the same time frame, his car also stopped working and he could not afford to fix it. So he was unemployed and had no car. But that does not stop a man like Bill Staton. He decided to use the next best form of transportation—his bike. He thought the best jobs were available in the Raleigh-Durham area, so he traveled 120-mile roundtrip each day by bicycle to look for work. He would carefully pack a shirt, tie, and slacks in a dry cleaner bag, and roll and pack it carefully into a backpack. Once he learned of a job opportunity, he would ride his bike to the location, change clothes in a restroom, and go to the interview. A shocked interviewer once said to him, "Didn't I see you earlier riding a bicycle?" When Bill told him that it was him, the interviewer said, "Now that is a determined man!"

Bill finally landed a job as a maintenance man at the hotel, and was riding thirty miles one way to work, five days a week. This meant he needed to leave for work about two hours before a shift started, and ride home at midnight. When I expressed my amazement, he simply said, "You have to do what you have to do."

Bill then shared with me his vision. He had already filed for a 501(c)3 in order to start a charity to build a community center in his area. He had already started speaking to people about getting grants, having involvement from Junior Achievement and neighborhood youth programs for kids to work and start their own businesses. He desires to make a difference in young people's lives so that they could truly achieve their dreams and stay out of trouble and off the streets.

Bill is also starting a small home-based business where he installs carpet vinyl and tile in his spare time. He has also started writing a book about his life experiences entitled *Angel's Two-Way Street.*

I told Bill that I was writing a book about special people and I would like to include him in one of the chapters. "I would be honored," he said. "Besides, you don't think it was coincidental that your air conditioner happened to be making a racket tonight did you? We were meant to meet, and it was all planned by a power neither one of us understands." Well said, Bill. Well said.

NOTES

1. **Treat others like you treat yourself.** "It's good to be good," Bill says, smiling. And you can feel even better about yourself. What have you done for someone else lately?

2. **People will do you wrong.** But don't let them bring you down. If you fall down, get right back up on your bike and just keep on going. The next service call you get may be hard, but just keep going.

3. **Look at life and just get it done.** Too many people say they can't or think they can't. Don't talk about it; just go do it.

4. **Persistence is key.** Many people would allow themselves to be unemployed, saying that they live in the wrong area. Bill did not make that a barrier. When his car broke down, he did not allow that to stop him from finding work. He just jumped on a bike.

WorkIT!

We know from our research that less than 3 percent of the population has clear articulated goals. Take out a piece of paper and calendar, or your journal, and write down specific goals to improve your customer service. It doesn't matter what time of year you do this—there is no time like the present.

_____

_____

_____

_____

_____

Identify in advance the barriers that may interfere with your ability to achieve great customer service goals. Think of ways to get around, over, and through those barriers. Now you have goals and a plan.

_____

_____

_____

_____

_____

_____

Once those goals and plans have been written down, take them and put a timeline to them. Take the timeline and post all of those dates on your calendar so you will see when they're due.

_____

_____

_____

_____

_____

How would you describe your overall attitude? If you would not describe your overall attitude as being completely 100 percent positive, that means you may need to consider changing it. Try to determine what is causing you to have a negative attitude and, most importantly, what you need to do to change it. This is critical to customer service.

_____

_____

_____

_____

_____

_____

CHAPTER 6

KATE HOLGATE:
THE PEOPLE MAGNET

I first met Kate Holgate when I was attending a National Speakers Association Conference. She was the one standing in the middle of the lobby surrounded by people as if she were somehow a human people magnet. We met in the lobby, and about every five minutes a different person would come over and say hello, give her a hug, and want to chat. She seemed to know everyone and everyone seemed to know her. That is just the kind of person Kate is.

When I first requested to do an interview with her, she asked, "Why me?" which illustrates her level of humility. Kate is in every way a "people person." She is customer service. All of us have known in our lifetime someone who is just a people person; they attract people like a magnet; they are a light bulb for the moths. When people are around them, they feel loved and appreciated. So how does someone develop this level of magnetism? I was wildly curious to learn the story behind the story.

Kate Holgate was born and raised in Charlotte, North Carolina, into, as she describes, a regular middle-class family—a mom and dad with two kids. Her mom was a copywriter at a large advertising agency and her dad repaired computer-operated equipment for large textile mills. She grew up in a tall family—she was five foot seven by the time she was ten years old. Her mom was six feet tall but always jokingly described herself as five foot twelve.

Kate grew up with one older brother and they were constantly in conflict with one another. They were different. Kate was born an extrovert and her brother was an introvert. He was tested and determined to be a genius. Due to his level of intelligence, he was put into a special school for gifted children, causing her and her brother to never attend school together until high school.

What's interesting about the situation is that Kate never really minded her brother having special skills and abilities, nor was she jealous of his intelligence. Part of that was due to her wonderful mother. Her mother always made it clear to her that she was not making any judgments nor was she comparing her to her brother. Once her mother joked with her, saying, "Bob might be smart, but he is alone and you have lots of other friends and many other gifts."

As with many kids, Kate's first outside influence was a remarkable teacher by the name of Ms. Fitzsimmons. Her teacher was an interesting person in that she was a body double for Maureen O'Sullivan, the actress in the *Tarzan* movies. She taught English classes and was quite the personality. At the end of the year, after the kids had begged, she actually entertained them by doing a Tarzan yell on the last day. What amazed Kate about this remarkable teacher was that on the first day of her class she asked Kate if she was any relation to Bob. After learning that he was her brother, the teacher came over, saw the look on Kate's face, knew that she was concerned, and said very quietly, "Just remember—you are you." That was a great relief to Kate and made her feel she could be herself and not be compared to her brother.

Growing up, Kate was definitely daddy's girl and he and Kate did many things together because of her innate curiosity. Her dad was a problem solver and a fixer, and if he was repairing the car and Kate walked by and asked, "What are you working on?" he would take the time to explain what he was working on and actually ask her to help. They worked on gardening, mechanics, and all sorts of projects around the house. He even taught her archery and let her shoot with the men in competition. It was overall a very pleasant childhood with highly supportive parents.

Unfortunately, everything in Kate's family changed at the age of twelve, and not for the better. During that time, her dad went from being a laid-back supportive dad to transforming into a religious fanatic overnight. Suddenly she went from being a good girl, to being called ugly names because she had long hair and had the audacity to wear lip-gloss. He would scream and yell at Kate and would even occasionally hit her.

Even though Kate found this tremendously disturbing, she still seemed to have a sense that her father had lost his mind and had gone off the deep end. To make things even more confusing, there were times when her dad would revert back to the old dad of the past and would be kind, nice, and supportive.

Then he would once again revert back to the fanatic when something set him off. I can imagine how incredibly confusing this must've been for a twelve-year-old.

Another teacher who had a big impact on Kate was Mr. Barnhart. Mr. Barnhart assigned Kate to make a movie about American history. She went to him because she was worried and said, "I don't think I can do it." He looked her in the eyes with a steely glance and said, "If you *want* to do it, you can do it—so do it." This gave Kate a tremendous boost of confidence because he believed in her. The version of her old father emerged and he took a great deal of pride in helping her with the film. They edited the film and added the sweet refrains of "America, The Beautiful" in the background. He was proud of her work.

Kate entered the high school years as a hippie—classic for that time, with long hair and bell-bottom jeans with an upside down Felix the cat patch on the back pocket. She wore zigzag shirts and openly admits she rebelled and started doing a lot of drugs. At the age of fifteen, she was suffering from a low level of self-esteem and attempted to kill herself because she did not know what she did wrong and why her father had abandoned her. As she described it to me, "I had a dad who was addicted to religion and a mom who was addicted to cigarettes." She still wonders how she escaped the addictions that seemed to plague her family.

At the age of sixteen, Kate met and married someone in order to escape the house and get away from her father. She married Michael, who was eighteen at the time, and who worked at a warehouse. They had fun "playing house" together, doing lots of drugs, and were way too immature to actually be married.

Her mom was also suffering during this time. The weekend that Kate got married, her mom moved into Kate's old bedroom, and not long after separated from her dad and divorced him. Seven years later Kate discovered that her own husband was cheating on her and they divorced as well. She had been married and divorced by the age of twenty-three.

Kate volunteered to run a local softball league, and at one of the games she met Dick. Dick was a clean-cut athletic type, and he asked her to marry him after only ten days of dating. Looking back on it, she realizes that she and Dick were not compatible in any way, shape, or form. She was marrying a man she thought her daddy would love. All Dick was interested in was sports—all he wanted to do was play or watch them. He was not very sensitive to her needs.

Shortly after that, Kate's mom started her own advertising agency. She asked Kate to work there as an account manager. Being the consummate people person, being the account manager was her dream job. She handled the technical accounts (after all, she had learned a lot about technology from her father growing up) and had the mind for it. Her mom handled the less technical accounts. Kate was just like her mom—everybody loved her, she was quite the character, and all of the vendors and suppliers loved her. When media representatives came to visit her to talk about buying advertising, she would take them out to the hallway and roll dice with them for discounts. Everyone loved Kate's mom. One of the most important lessons that her mother taught her was, "Do not judge me by my success; judge me by my attempts."

Around this time in her life, Kate sat down for a talk with her father. He asked her to forgive him for how he treated her all of those years and humbly apologized. He also told her that he would take it all back if he could. Ironically, he still remained a religious fanatic for the rest of his life.

Her mom was diagnosed with lung cancer in August of 1988 and died very quickly in November of the same year. Kate was devastated that her best friend, her mother, business partner, and mentor had passed away. She did not know what she was going to do with the rest of her life. She had worked there for eight years. Her marriage to Dick had already begun to unravel too. The stress of all that had happened was just too much. She had no support system and knew she could not live life with a husband like that.

Shortly after her mother died, she was stressed out and grieving. One day she got a call from her cousin Reggie, who asked her to come to Florida to hang out, go to the beach, lay in the sun, and figure out what she wanted to do next. She took him up on his offer and went to the beach to reevaluate her life. A few days after she arrived at Reggie's house, she reconnected with his brother, Rick, whom she had not seen in twenty years.

Rick walked into the house, took one look at Kate, smiled, and said, "Well, Kate looks like puberty was pretty nice to you." She fell in love on the spot and moved to Sarasota eight months later. Rick and Kate have now been married for twenty-one years. Kate laughs when she tells people she married her cousin, whom she calls her *cousband*—saying, "I am Southern, after all."

Seeking a creative outlet similar to an advertising agency, she started working for the Asolo Theater Company and then went from there to the FSU/Asolo Acting Conservatory. After working there for fourteen years, the school hired a new dean and he fired Kate.

After learning there was going to be a fundraiser to benefit hurricane victims, and while working on the volunteer committee, Kate suggested that Linda Larsen (who was a graduate of the conservatory) and her husband emcee the evening event. At the event, talking backstage, Linda asked Kate, "What are you doing lately? I need you to come and work for me." Kate agreed to go to work with Linda, who was a professional speaker. She fell in love with the world of professional speakers because she was able to apply all of her skill sets.

After a few years, sadly, Kate had to quit her job and leave town to take care of her brother who needed a liver transplant. After she nursed her brother through his illness, she decided to start a business of her own, managing other professional speakers. She was lucky because Linda had taught her everything she knew about the speaking business. She loved having her own business.

When asked why she does what she does today, her answer is straightforward and instant: "I have the best, most perfect job in the world. I get to be around people I love and love working with. I also feel a very strong need be part of something important. You see, I know that I am part of something important because the speakers that I represent are out there changing the world."

When people learn about Kate's childhood, they tell her they are sorry. Kate, however, is not sorry because her childhood made her who she is today. Even though she lost her mother, if her mother had not died, she would not have reconnected with Rick, gotten a job at the conservatory, met Linda, and been pushed into starting her own business. "You have to push through the stuff in life because what you learn eventually is that there is a reason why everything happens," she says.

"I am in the groove," says Kate, "and I can't wait to see what tomorrow brings, having a great husband like Rick and wonderful people around me, whom I love." It sounds silly, but when you talk to Kate on the phone, you can hear the words, and as corny as it may sound, you can also feel the love.

NOTES

1. **Stuff happens.** It is not what happens to you that shapes who you are, it's how you react to what happens to you. Kate could have certainly given up when faced with adversity in her life, but she did not—she kept going.

2. **Work with people you love.** Too many times we choose to work with people who are not positive, not motivated, and not a positive influence in our life. Kate has decided whom she will and will not work with, and that has had a big impact on both her and her work. When she says, "I love my speakers," she really means every one of those words.

3. **Be able to laugh.** Kate has the remarkable ability to laugh and is always joking around and using southern humor. When describing her husband who cheated, she said, "He wanted me to share my bed with some other woman—and, mama don't play that way!" You just have to laugh at her refreshing sense of humor.

4. **Be persistent.** Kate's mom taught her the value of persistence and hard work; stick to what it is that you dream of doing. Often we give up too soon.

5. **Have perspective.** Even at a young age, Kate was wise enough to understand the why behind her

father's fanaticism and realized it was a form of psychosis, not something that was her fault. She was able to analyze it on a different level.

WorkIT!

Take out a piece of paper and a pen, and make a list of the things you love that are part of your work. Yes, I said the word *love*, not *like*. If the list of things you love is a significant list, then congratulations. If the list of things that you love is short, then figure out how you can love them or go do something else.

_____

_____

_____

_____

_____

Make a list of all the customer service challenges you're facing in your work life currently. On the left side, list the challenges; on the right side, list the perspectives of how other people may see it. This may help you analyze a challenge from a different perspective.

_____

_____

_____

_____

_____

_____

To be great at customer service, you need to have a sense of humor. To develop a better sense of humor, make a list of things you can do this week to help make you laugh more. It may be watching a funny TV show, movie, or reading a funny book; or it may come by being with other people who are known as being funny.

_____

_____

_____

_____

_____

_____

Do something new—at least for new discoveries and opportunities. Decide each week some new social or professional opportunity you can get involved with that will possibly help stimulate your thinking and boost your morale. Remember that when you are fired up and excited, it comes through in customer service.

_____

_____

_____

_____

_____

CHAPTER 7

NICOLAS RODRIGUES: DRIVING AMERICA

NICK Rodrigues was born and raised in Cuba. His father was a farmer with a lot of land. When Fidel Castro came to power and things got bad for the people of Cuba, Nick's father wanted to escape with his family and come to America. The Castro regime found out about this and deemed Nick's father and one of Nick's brothers enemies of the state, putting them both in jail. His brother stayed in jail for three years and his father for ten.

Nick went to school in Cuba until the sixth grade. Then he had to go to work in construction, doing hard labor, to make money and help his family survive while his father and brother were imprisoned.

In 1980, six years after Nick's father was released from prison, Castro opened the gates and allowed all political prisoners (plus many others in prison) and anyone else to leave Cuba. When he was just sixteen years old, Nick—along with his mother, father, oldest brother, and his oldest brother's wife and three children—came to the United States of America.

You may remember the Mariel boatlift, which was a mass exodus of Cubans who departed from Cuba's Mariel Harbor for the United States between April 15 and October 31, 1980. This was brought on by a sharp downturn in the Cuban economy that led to internal tensions and a bid by nearly 10,000 Cubans to gain asylum at the Peruvian embassy. Because of this, the Cuban government announced that anyone who wanted to leave could do so, and the exodus by boat began. Cuban Americans organized it with the agreement of Fidel Castro. As many as 125,000 Cubans made it to the shores of south Florida.

Nick and his family were among them. They traveled on a forty-eight-foot boat with fifty passengers for sixteen hours in extremely rough seas. To this day, Nick remembers it well. They finally reached America, landing in Key West. The U.S. government and the Red Cross had set up a station where the boats were landing. As people arrived, they were helped off the ships and given blankets, hot food, and water and soap for showers. They were also given shelter and beds to sleep in for the night.

Early the next morning at eight o'clock, buses transported the Cuban arrivals to the Key West Airport, where they boarded a plane bound for Sparta, Wisconsin. When they landed in Sparta, school buses awaited them, and they were driven forty-five minutes to Fort McCoy, an active Army installation.

At Fort McCoy, the Cuban refugees were housed in Army barracks and cared for while the immigration process took place. Nick and his family were there for one month. During the immigration process they tried to contact family members living in the United States who would vouch for each Cuban and agree to house them and help them start their new life in America.

Nick's family had a cousin living in New Jersey at the time. Once immigration services confirmed this and the cousin agreed to sponsor them, they were put on a plane bound for New Jersey. Nick and his family lived with his cousin for one month before Nick, his father, and his brother found jobs and two apartments to house their two families. They were on their way to life in America. Their dream was coming true!

Nick and his father worked at a dairy plant. He worked the milk-packing machine and continued to work there for six years. After three years they had saved up enough money to buy a house where Nick and his parents could live.

He found a new job with a local limo company using his own car and did this for six more years. During those six years, he saved enough money to eventually go out on his own and start his own limo business. He wanted to go out on his own because he loves what he does. He loves helping people get to where they need to go. He loves to do this in an efficient way while making his customers comfortable, relaxed, and sure they will get to where they need to go without any stress or drama. At first, it was just Nick and his car. But then he acquired a stretch limo, and then another town car, and soon another. Nick has now been running his own limo business for sixteen years.

Seventeen years after Nick left Cuba on that infamous Mariel flotilla, he went back to visit his remaining family there. While he was there, he met a woman by the name of Damarys. During subsequent trips back to Cuba, they fell in love and were finally married. Nick came back to the United States without her to try to get the papers processed for her to move to America so she could live with him. Damarys was also pregnant with their first child.

With his family's support and the help of professionals, it took Nick four long years to get the documents approved to allow his wife and their young daughter to move to the United States. Today, they live in New Jersey, happy to be in America, working hard and raising their now twelve-year-old daughter together. Nick's eighty-five-year-old mother also lives with them, and his oldest brother lives with his family in Tampa, Florida. Nick also has an older daughter and a son from a previous marriage, who live in the United States. Nick's father passed away in 2007 at the age of eighty-seven.

As for Nick's limo company, it is doing great. You can often see him at the bottom of the escalator near the baggage claim in any of the three New York City area airports, awaiting a passenger with a great big smile and his "I am at your service" attitude. He often wears his beret to help identify him. And if I must say, he looks pretty smashing in it!

His attitude toward his job, why he still loves it and how he performs it, has not changed. It has only gotten better with time. Most of Nick's customers are repeat customers and he has many referrals from his regulars. Nick makes sure to call everyone by name. He is always friendly, happy, upbeat, and courteous. He tracks their flights to make sure he or his people are always on time. He keeps his customer information on file to make the payment process efficient. And he e-mails the receipt to them so the entire process is seamless. Nick stays up-to-date with technology to set him apart from many other small limo companies. He told me that staying small means he controls how well he and his team perform their job and how well they can give the best customer service possible.

I asked Nick about what motivates him. He said, "I want to always do my best, improve myself. I don't want to stay in the same place; I want to get ahead. I like to work, I like to work hard, and I like to make my customers happy. And I am happy too." Doesn't this sound similar to many of our ancestors who came to America since 1776? As Warren Buffet once said during an interview with Charlie Rose, "I was born lucky, I was born in America." Nick told me that he owes it all to his father's wish for a better life for his family. "My father felt really American." And he was.

NOTES

1. **Be willing to be brave.** Be brave enough to speak up for your human rights.

2. **Have a dream.** Nick's father dreamed of a better life for his family. Nick had the same dream for his family. Focusing on that dream and working toward their goals helped Nick and his father attain it.

3. **Ask for help when you need it.** There are always many people who are willing to help others. Take the help when you need it, and remember to pay it back someday too.

4. **Go back to your roots.** Sometimes you need to go back to your roots to find the right person to complete you. In Nick's case, it took a trip back to Cuba after seventeen years to find the love of his life.

5. **Hold onto love.** Love is, and always will be, undefeated. Nick never gave up though it took him four long years to bring his wife and daughter to America.

6. **Have style.** Wearing something that gives you a signature style, like Nick's beret, can make people remember you and also identify you in a crowd.

7. **Work on you.** If you don't want to stay in the same place, **try** to improve yourself, and start by doing your best.

8. **Embrace change.** Don't fight it. Embracing change and being proud of the country you live in can feel really great!

WorkIT!

Do you have short-term, mid-term, and long-term goals for yourself? Does your company have the same?

_____

_____

_____

_____

_____

_____

If not, write down three short-term goals to be accomplished this week. Write down three mid-term goals to be accomplished this month, and three long-term goals to be accomplished this year. Look at this list every day, and work on one item at a time, focusing on each until it is accomplished.

Short-term goals:

1. _____

_____

_____

2. _____

_____

_____

3. _____

_____

_____

Mid-term goals:

1. _____

_____

_____

2. _____

_____

_____

3. _____

_____

_____

Long-term goals:

1. _____

_____

_____

2. _____

_____

_____

3. _____

_____

_____

Do you have a mentor or someone you can go to and ask for help with something you wish to accomplish?

_____

_____

_____

_____

_____

If not, get one. Asking others to help you will help. Remember to repay them in some small way and to help others along the way too.

_____

_____

_____

_____

_____

Do you have your own unique style that may identify you or set you apart?

_____

_____

_____

_____

This is not for everyone, but if it is you, try it. Always dress in your own style and be true to it. People may remember you better by a style that is uniquely yours. If you need to find a style to call your own, there are style experts in most retail stores who can help you. Go to your favorite store and ask.

Are the customer service systems you use efficient? If not, why? How can they be improved?

_____

_____

_____

_____

_____

Do your customers or clients refer you or your company to others? Why? If they do not, why not?

_____

_____

_____

_____

_____

CHAPTER 8

JOE FLEMING:
SKYCAP WITH TRUE SPIRIT

IT is hard enough to have to be at work every morning at four o'clock, but to want to arrive an hour early at three is downright unusual. It's not unusual for Joe Fleming, however. Joe arrives at work at three o'clock every morning along with a few of the other guys so they can get their minds right for the day. During this hour, Joe thinks about life, about the day, and relaxes and meditates. Joe told me he is very disciplined—he has never been late for his job, not one day, ever!

Joe Fleming is a skycap at the Fort Lauderdale Airport in Florida. He works for a company called Bags Incorporated. Joe and his coworkers are responsible for checking in, tagging, and picking up the bags for Delta Airlines curbside. Not an easy task at best, and then throw in the weather elements and the passenger personalities and you have a really challenging job. But Joe does it all with professionalism, ease, eloquence, and a gentle "can do" manner.

Let's be honest—this is a hard job that many people wouldn't really want in the first place. Once someone had the job, he or she wouldn't want to go to work early, but Joe does. He is motivated to do a good job in an efficient, caring manner. He loves giving great service to his customers.

When you meet him for the first time, and he takes over checking you in and taking care of your luggage, you know he is special. You know your bags will get to where they need to go. This man really cares! He has energy, is fast-paced, and has a passion for what he is doing.

I met Joe in 1972 when he had just moved to Fort Lauderdale from Atlanta and got the skycap position, at that time with Aircraft Services International. He was the same on that first day as he is today. Joe Fleming is a genuine gentleman who does his job well with a caring attitude. It shows and it shines right through, even at four in the morning. In all the years I have known Joe Fleming, he has never ever, ever changed. He is true to himself. He loves what he does and lets it show. He is proud to be of service to the people he helps.

Joe was born in Eastman, Georgia, and started school there. His mother raised him on her own; his father was not in his life. At ninety-six years old, Joe's mother is still an upbeat and a happy person. He says that it was his mother who molded him—she made the difference in his life.

In 1962, Joe moved to Florida to go to a trade school to learn how to be a computer repair technician. Having difficulty finding a job after school, he moved back to Atlanta in 1965 to accept a position as a warehouse manager. He worked there until 1972, when he moved back to Fort Lauderdale and got the skycap position. He worked two full-time jobs back then. While he worked as a skycap, he also worked for Modern Age Furniture in Miami, making sure the right furniture got on the right truck going out for deliveries.

Joe married his wife, Betty, in 1975. They have been married for thirty-eight years now and have four daughters and one son. Their oldest daughter, Selina, and youngest daughter, Monica, graduated from Florida A&M University in Tallahassee, Florida, and Monica is still attending graduate school there. Their second daughter graduated from the University of Florida with a master's degree in education and is a teacher in Gainesville, Florida. Jennifer, their third daughter, works as a childcare professional in Palm Bay, Florida. Joe's son, Ralston, lives in Atlanta, Georgia, and is a barber and an entrepreneur.

When I ask Joe's friends about him, they say he is a person of value. He doesn't just do, he really does, and he believes in what he does no matter what it is. He is passionate about all of life. Joe says to me, "Being a black man is hard, but you can be a good citizen." His dear mother, his teachers, and his whole community raised him. He was taught to be "honest, be straight in what you do, don't cheat, no smoking, no drinking, and no cursing.

As for Joe's children, he gives them true, genuine love and tries to set an example for them. He does charity work feeding the homeless and sits on the board of Human Resource Development, Inc., which helps first-time homebuyers with the process.

No matter the time of morning, the weather, airline delays, or the amount of baggage to be checked, Joe Fleming is always the same. He is always consistently pleasant and efficient. He loves people. In his job, he tries to be as kind, happy, and upbeat as possible to his flying public. He says, "When you deal with so many people every single day, you have to be kind because you have no idea what they are going through, what they might have been through, and why they are flying.

After interviewing Joe and reflecting on the many dozens of times he met me at the curbside, I realized he has always called me by my name, always greeted me with a smile, and is always ready to get the job done. I can hear it in my head: "Hello, how are you this morning?" and "Where are you going today?" And for the good-byes, "Good-bye, have a great trip and see you next time. Give my best to your family." Thank you, Joe, and see you next flight.

NOTES

1. **Get up and be early.** It helps to get where you are going early to have time to get your mind ready for the task at hand.

2. **Do it right.** No matter what the job is, do it well and efficiently.

3. **Always listen to your mother.** Listen to your mother, know what you really love about her, and try to be like her.

4. **Have friends.** A true support system can be far-reaching. It can include teachers as well as people in your local community.

5. **Lead the way.** Be an example to others and let your true goodness shine through. Others will notice and will be changed by this goodness even though they may not know what this goodness is.

6. **Serve others.** No matter how busy you are and how many hours you work, make time for others and be charitable to them. Teach others to do the same.

7. **Love the world.** Love is a gift we must give to one another.

WorkIT!

Do you plan your time on your calendar to get to where you are going at least ten minutes early? When possible, make that twenty to thirty minutes early. Planning this way allows you to reflect on the task at hand and be prepared for things that go wrong. Dependable people do this every single day.

_____

_____

_____

_____

_____

Can you list the people who have influenced you as a young person? Pick three and write down three things about each of them that you would like to copy. Put these attributes into every task you do. Write them down on your daily task list, and build them into every document you prepare and conversation you have.

1. _____

_____

_____

2. _____

_____

_____

3. _____

_____

_____

Do you ask others for their help? If not, why? If you are struggling with an issue or are just stuck on something, make a list of people you can ask for help, opinions, and guidance. Be frank with them, telling them exactly what you are doing and what you are asking of them. Take notes. Try each one of their tactics and find at least one that works. If you find one, don't stop there—try all of them. There are often several ways to solve a problem.

_____

_____

_____

_____

_____

Do you work at getting your attitude right each day? Practice doing this each day before work. See yourself being successful, doing your job with a smile, and a great attitude. See yourself happy, accomplishing what you need to, and even going beyond that. See your customers saying yes, agreeing, and thanking you for helping them. See your customers buying what you are selling and being happy about it.

_____

_____

_____

_____

_____

Do you make time each week for a person in need? If not, find someone who can use your help and give it. Block out this time on your calendar, weekly or at least monthly, and take the time to help him or her. In turn, ask that person to do one small favor for you. Try it!

_____

_____

_____

_____

_____

_____

CHAPTER 9

PEARL DEERY:
PEARLS OF WISDOM

HAVE you ever seen the movie *The Flying Nun*? I watched it again recently, and it reminded me of Pearl Deery. She is not only a remarkably unique person in her own right, but she also certainly fits her name. She is so very *dear* to this world in so many ways. She has a lot of energy and is motivated and dynamic—you expect her to fly! She just has that kind of special quality about her. Talk about real customer service. And yes, Pearl is a nun. I know you are thinking of the stereotypical nun, wearing a habit and robes, but that is not Pearl. She is a real character and a true individual. Some might say she is even a real "hoot!"

Pearl just turned sixty-one, and when she became a nun, things were much different. She was attracted to the life of being a sister when she was just eighteen years old. She had wonderful memories of her own education and liked to help people find their passions in life—to service people, if you will. Her family was supportive and said, "Try it, Pearl; try being a nun. Teach, and if you like it, you can stay with it." Pearl loved it and is still a nun to this day. She truly fell in love with her calling. How many people love what they do? How many people love their work? How many people feel their work is a calling? Not many I have met.

Pearl started in a convent in a small town in Ireland called Dundalk. The town is situated where the Castleton River flows into the Dundalk Bay and is equidistant between Belfast and Dublin. She was never allowed to leave the convent and couldn't even go to stay with her mother when her father passed away. It was the strict way of the convent back then, and she accepted it. Over the years things have changed in the world of nuns, and now Pearl wears regular clothes (but usually not too stylish), drives a car, uses a computer to send e-mails, and has a life like most of us. Yes, nuns now have technology too.

Pearl is so interesting to talk to about life because she has a simple, almost naïve perspective of the world. Her viewpoint is quite refreshing and most entertaining. Although her main work in the sisterhood is education and nursing, for many years Pearl has served teens through education and youth work events.

At the age of fifty, she was asked to go and live in Nigeria for two years to work as a teacher in a tiny village in the middle of nowhere. Now imagine, she had never left Dundalk in her entire life, never been out in the world, never been on a plane, and she had agreed to move to Nigeria for *two* years! Now that takes faith and a love of what you do.

In Nigeria, Pearl was in constant fear of dying of some disease or a car accident. This never stopped her, however, and she never turned back. One night she was traveling down a dirt road with her Nigerian driver, whom she was quite fond of and who became a very important part of her life while she was there.

As they were driving along one day, they saw a dead body on the side of the road. The driver was afraid to stop for fear he would be accused of murder. Pearl, however, insisted that they do something and got the driver to go to the nearest police station to report what they had discovered. Pearl then led the police officer and the driver back to pick up the body. She said she couldn't tolerate the thought that this man wouldn't be buried with dignity, and so the man was. Perhaps the real reason Pearl was sent "with faith" and to serve in Nigeria was for this man. While her driver lacked courage, Pearl had conviction and put aside any worry about being accused. She had to do the right thing and she did.

She survived the two years in Nigeria without injury, but when she arrived back home in Ireland, she was in a terrible car accident and broke her neck. Fortunately, she fully recovered with no long-term impact, which is amazing in itself.

Pearl is the kindest, nicest, and most amazing lady in so many ways. She sees things with different eyes and loves and lives life to its fullest. Everything seems new to her. She has a great sense of humor too. Her friend Leo Sullivan asked her once what she was going to wear to a family wedding, and she replied, "I have two suits: a blue one for funerals and a pink one for weddings." Her friend Leo replied, "I hope you will wear the pink one," and she did, with sandals! Pearl says, "Being a nun allows me to wear whatever is comfortable, because people will say, 'Oh, she's a nun; what does she know?'" This also shows her insight into human nature.

Today, Pearl is still a teacher in Ireland and a volunteer with the Apple Tree Foundation, where young people can go to get in touch with themselves and their individual gifts of creativity. She has also helped to get much-needed funding for the Youth Café, where kids can go to experience music, dance, films, and exhibitions. For many of the kids, it is the first time they can experience any of the arts live. Kids love energy and honesty, especially kids who carry a lot of pain, often from their own families.

Pearl has a diverse variety of friends, including fellow nuns, others who were nuns but left the sisterhood, married couples, and colleagues. Her friends say that she is very much a "people person." She enriches her life by being busy with the community. She takes joy in living with people through their ups and downs and often can help them through it all. Pearl sees this as serving...or as she says, "giving real personal customer service."

Though she is sometimes overworked, she says, "My body is my friend, and when it tells me to slow down, I do." How many of us listen to our own body's advice? Not many, I am sure. She says she could not be anything but what she is, because she believes we are who we are "inside out." Pearl is a great believer that when we "work together," none of us is the greater or lesser, but we are all equally important to the greater good. We are all equal in everything we do together. Don't you think Pearl's ideas could be useful in many places in the world? I have no doubt.

There is no better example of serving others than Pearl Deery. Sometimes we donate our time, our belongings, or our money to charities or people who need help. Pearl, on the other hand, has dedicated her entire *life* to serving others. She has devoted her work and her time to the greater good to help others and to serve them with all she has in herself to enrich their lives. Pearl Deery is a rare pearl and the rarest of all the "human pearls," who bring beauty and light to the world by serving.

NOTES

1. **Try it; you might love it.** Often we need a nudge from others who know us to try out a new career. Sometimes others see in us what we do not see in ourselves. Maybe we should trust the insight of others more often.

2. **When opportunity knocks, go for it.** Nothing ventured, nothing gained. Sometimes opportunity comes to us for what seems like one reason but ends up being for another totally unexpected reason.

3. **Laugh at yourself. (Even if you are a nun!)** Finding humor in yourself and the world will make others open up to you, talk to you more, and learn from you. *You* will also learn from them.

4. **You're never too old.** Age is only a number. You are never too old to try something new, move to a new place, or take on a new challenge. Your youth and vibrancy are determined by the people you hang out with, how you think, how you act, and how much you learn from others and your experiences.

5. **Follow your instincts and do what it right.** Like Pearl with the body on the side of the road, do what you know is morally right in every instance. You may have been put into a situation for reasons beyond your own understanding.

WorkIT!

Do you listen to what others say about what they see in you and how they view your talents? If others are not saying things about you, ask them what they see and get their read on *you*. Then, take their advice.

_____

_____

_____

_____

_____

_____

Do you look and listen when opportunity knocks? Do you really listen with your third ear to what is being said (what is *really* meant to what is being said) to opportunities that come your way? These usually come for a reason. Seize the moment and remember to ask questions and follow through.

_____

_____

_____

_____

_____

_____

Humor is a great antidote to life's troubles. Do you use humor to get you through tough times? How do you use it? Give examples of where you go in your head to get you though.

_____

_____

_____

_____

_____

Make a list of the things you want to do and the places you want to go this year. Write down at least three goals, and then make a plan to do everything on your list within twelve months. Be very specific when making plans and setting goals. The more specific you are, the greater the chance you will accomplish these things.

_____

_____

_____

_____

_____

_____

_____

_____

_____

CHAPTER 10

GOLDIE BROWN: SLIPCOVER MAVEN

PERHAPS Goldie Lee Brown got her name because of the color of her hair. She certainly looked like a Goldie: her hair was a lovely, golden tone; her skin was peaches and cream; and she had the youngest, clearest speaking voice you could imagine.

Goldie Brown was born in Elk Fork, Kentucky, and moved to Logan, West Virginia, during high school. She started sewing at the age of fourteen and was self-taught. She married young and had a son shortly thereafter. One day, the baby spit up on her couch, and the spot would not come out. Being young and not having a lot of money, she could not afford to have the couch recovered. So she decided to try to make a slipcover for it, and that was where it all started.

Her mother-in-law thought she did a "really good job" with the slipcover and asked if she would make one for her. Goldie did. Soon thereafter, others were asking Goldie to make slipcovers for them too. Word got out around the town, and before Goldie knew it, a business was born. She was working almost every day, making slipcovers for friends, neighbors, relatives, and eventually strangers. A local store called Stone and Thomas heard about her and recommended her to customers who bought fabric from them.

She eventually moved to Louisville, Kentucky, with her family where she once again started a very successful business, pleasing customers and covering furniture every day. She also made covers for pillows and anything else that needed to be covered. She was an expert zipper lady too.

Goldie's work was fairly priced, always diligent and on time, precise, professionally done, and so good it was often hard to tell that what was covering the couch was a slipcover at all; you might have thought it was upholstered. She was that good! She collected and used three sewing machines, all Singers. One of them was about sixty years old, which was her favorite. "It still works just fine," she told me.

Once, a client who had work for Goldie called her to ask when she was able to start the project. Goldie said, "It will be a few more days. I am still at Sue's house, and the work is a little more than I thought here. I think I have covered everything in the house except the cat!"

The beauty of what Goldie did is that she gave the ultimate in customer service. She went to the customer! She would go to the client's home with her sewing machine and the tools of her trade in tow and did the work right there. Her customer's furniture did not have to be hauled around. Goldie liked it that way because she also didn't have the clean up at home, she had low overhead, and sometimes she even got lunch. Smart.

Goldie did not use scissors or measuring tape when cutting and sizing fabric to fit. Yes, that's right; she just used her hands. When you saw her do this, it could be a little unnerving, especially if you had spent $100 on a yard of fabric. You might think, "What the heck is she doing? Does she really know what she is doing?"

You see, what she did was take the bolt of fabric and unroll it, and with her arms spread wide, she visually measured one, two, three feet of fabric up against the couch or chair to fit it for sizing. Once she had determined how much she was going to use for the piece, she took the end of the fabric and ripped it with her hands. Goldie said, "Ripping the fabric is a lot faster, and you also get a much straighter line then cutting." Who knew? Goldie did.

She then went to work on her sewing machine, often set up on a card table or dining table right in the room where the furniture was to be covered, zipping along at record speed with the precision and vision of an artist. It was clear that Goldie loved what she did. You could see it in the quality of her work, in her unending energy, and in her focus and passion for what she was doing.

After her husband passed away in Louisville, Goldie moved to Fort Lauderdale, Florida, where she lived and worked with her successful business for many years. Then she moved back to Louisville to be closer to her sister and family. Shortly after settling in, she once again established her business and did well. Many of her clients from Florida kept calling her, asking when she could come to visit and do some work for them. A few clients even got together and paid for a ticket to fly her back to Florida. Goldie loved this, and of course she did the work.

She once had a Florida client call to request another slip-cover for his couch. The old one she had made needed to be replaced. He asked if he could send her the old slipcover so she could make another one just like it. She said, "I am afraid not, it would be better and faster if you sent the couch!" Goldie explained that it was more difficult and time-consuming to disassemble a slipcover and make a pattern than it was just to start from scratch.

Goldie re-covered his couch on her very next visit to Florida. She always does what she says she will. She always remembers and honors her existing customers by getting to them quickly. She follows up and follows through consistently with every single one of her customers. She never takes one for granted—ever!

Goldie just loved what she did for many reasons. She said, "It gives me a good living, and I get to go to a different place almost every day, see different homes, each with a different décor, and I get to meet nice people along the way too." Her philosophy was, "The more you go and do, the more you get to do."

Goldie was still going, doing, and getting to go and do more every day. The day before we talked to her about her life, she told us she finally sold her car and now her clients picked her up and took her to their homes to do her work. It worked nicely for Goldie.

She was born on December 13, 1913, making her ninety-six years young and still going strong. She had outlived her husband, her son, her sister, and many of her friends, but her verve and vigor for life remained a wonderful gift to all who knew and loved her. She had covered a lot of furniture, traveled a lot of miles, and certainly changed our lives for the better just by being herself. She always gave the very best customer service and always did her very best work.

Goldie Lee Brown passed away on November 11, 2009. She will definitely be missed by all who had the pleasure of knowing her lovely spirit.

NOTES

1. **Keep moving.** The more you do, the more you get to do. An object in motion tends to stay in motion. If you keep up your energy and momentum, things happen.

2. **Know what you are good at.** Like Goldie, find out what you like to do and are good at. Then do it. Once you find some success, build on that and stay the course.

3. **Find your niche.** Once you find out what you're good at, find a way to really focus on it. Niche businesses are always needed. Try to find a niche that few others fill.

4. **Try to do it faster and perhaps easier.** Like Goldie ripping fabric instead of cutting it, try to find a way to do what you are doing more efficiently. This can save time and usually money. Time often equals money.

5. **Produce with quality.** Regardless of what you do or make, do it with the very best quality you can. People will recommend you, remember you, and call you again and again. People will remember you for it.

WorkIT!

Are you are looking for a new business opportunity? If so, niche businesses often work. Offering a service or product that is needed by consumers, and perhaps hard to find, are best. Look around your community and make a list of the types of businesses that are in cluster retail areas.

_____

_____

_____

_____

_____

Decide what business you might be able to perform well in. Look around your community at other cluster retail areas that might need that particular business you think you are good at, and go from there (i.e., there might be a successful car wash on the east side of town but none on the west side of town). List the opportunities, research them, and then go for it.

_____

_____

_____

_____

_____

Regardless of your type of business, remember to make it easy for the customer to get what you're offering. List ways that you can improve on how you deliver what you do to your customers.

_____

_____

_____

_____

_____

Are you honest with your customers if doing what they want is not the best way to do it? List examples of when this has happened and write down how you will handle it next time.

_____

_____

_____

_____

_____

Part of giving good customer service is memory of past experiences with and recognition of each customer (if you can't remember, keep good files). Start remembering and calling your customers by name. It is an easy thing to do if you use the association technique (i.e., let's say a person's name is Mrs. Appletree. She has a round face like an apple and she is tall. Remember these two things and you will start remembering her name).

Try it daily. The more you do this, the better you will get at it. People like to be remembered and like to be called by their name. I had a landscaping service for twenty-five years and the owner addressed me by my name every single time we had an encounter. It showed respect. It showed that he valued my business and I liked it.

CHAPTER 11

BEATRIZ FARLAND:
BE INSPIRED, BE GIVING,
BE POSITIVE

BEATRIZ Farland, or "B" as she prefers to be called, was born in Chicago and moved to south Florida at the age of four. She grew up there, raised a family, and has a fitness studio that changes people lives for the better. You might say she is motivated to help people get healthy, and she does it all in a professional and passionate way.

Let's face it, most of us don't leap at the chance to take a spinning or Pilates class first thing in the morning, but B's students do. What's her secret? She believes in herself, and through this she inspires others to be the best they can be too. She radiates a can-do attitude. She instills this in her students and is there for them when they need her. This is what we call serious, compassionate customer service that can change a life.

B loves to dance and was on her high school dance team. After she graduated from high school, she started at Broward Community College (BCC). She joined a gym at the age of seventeen and started teaching step aerobics classes the same year.

When B took her first step class, she loved it. Like dance, it was physical and rhythmic, which seemed so natural to her. The step instructor thought B was so good she put her in a contest with sixty other girls from the fitness center. Although B really did not want to enter the contest, she was persuaded, and she ended up winning. From there she gained a sense of confidence.

One day, the step instructor did not show up for a class, and the owner of the center asked B if she would teach it. B said, "Oh no, I'm too shy." The owner said, "You have to." B considered it and thought, "What a great opportunity to get over my fears, do something I love, and be able to share that love with others." She agreed to teach the step class. Reflecting back on that day, B says she was awful and she was scared, but she remembers saying to herself, "I can do this." And she did it. Part of why this worked for B is that she has an instant rapport with people. People like her, trust her, and will follow her advice. Her love and passion for fitness and what she does helps make this work, as well as her sheer talent.

When B is scared or shy, has a really big challenge, or thinks she can't do something, she has always had something deep inside of her that tells her, "Try it. You can do this and you will succeed." This is an inner driving voice that B uses to challenge herself and her clients. "We all have so much more potential in us; we just have to take ourselves out of our comfort zones and have a positive outlook to find that out." What B offers to her students is what I like to call "intangible customer service." She gives her students hope and belief in themselves that they can do it.

Beatriz loved the experience of teaching her first fitness class so much so that she got certified while going to college. After two years at BCC, B went to Florida State University (FSU), where she tried out to become one of the university's group exercise instructors. This was the first time she had to audition to be an instructor, and she was up against a large and tough group of instructors who all wanted this amazing opportunity. When she got the position, she was so happy and excited. She taught classes to more than sixty students at a time and says it was one of the best experiences she has ever had in her career. She gained tremendous confidence during her teaching years at FSU.

After college, B worked at several fitness studios with the dream that someday she would have her own. She wanted to create a place "that is not competitive, where people think and feel like I do." B thought to herself, "I can do this!" Her goal was to give each client a feeling of positive energy and positive support. Again, this is intangible customer service that B is known for. She wanted to create a place that focused on a balanced life: a space where there was great personal attention, where people felt good and safe, and where everyone knew your name—a fitness studio that inspired confidence and trust.

In January 2010, B did just that, and Studio BE opened. The name came to her one day as she was out running alone; she thought about what the studio would be about. Then it came to her: "Be strong, be inspiring, be happy, be balanced, be giving"—basically, just "BE." Studio BE has a menu of classes:

Spinning, Pilates, Boot Camp, Xtend Ballet Barre, and more. B says that the Xtend Ballet Barre class is like "Pilates amped up." With this class, she feels like she has come full circle back to her first fitness love: dance.

She inspires her students to try, to feel like they can do it, and to find the voice inside of them that says, "Let out all the stuff inside that is holding you back from doing this: you *can* do this." "Stay away from any negative voices or people that hold you back," B says. "This is your life, and we all deserve to be as happy and healthy as we possibly can be."

B's clients are like family to her; she says they inspire her more than she inspires them. They inspired her to do her first marathon, her first 150-mile bike ride, her first half Ironman, and to open her own studio, because they knew she could do it. She is grateful to all the people who have come and gone, and who continue to be in her life—those who have helped her along her journey.

In April 2010 B gave birth to her first child, Sebastian, who is the love of her life. She found out she was pregnant the same week she decided to open Studio BE. She feels there was a higher reason these two things happened at the same time. Throughout her entire pregnancy, she continued to be active and gave classes until two weeks before her son was born. It was a wonderful healthy pregnancy.

B says of exercise, "This stuff really works." Even after having a nine-pound baby and a C-section, she recovered very quickly. She was back to work, back to working out stronger than ever before, and back to teaching, guiding, and encouraging her students with her intangible customer service. The experience of having a baby and all the things the body goes through during and after has enabled her to help other women having babies too. She now knows what it takes to get in shape and all that it takes to stay there.

B has seen so many fitness folks doing too much, overdoing workouts, and injuring themselves. People often overdo fitness because it allows them to emotionally run away from something, and the fitness high makes them feel good for a while. Through her years of experience, she has learned that exercise is a key to being happy, but that overdoing anything is never good. She makes it her goal to teach balance and safety while exercising. She teaches that exercise = happiness = balance. Life to B is about balance, health, family, and career—all in that order.

She often talks as she teaches her spinning classes, and it is often self-talk that she shares with her students. She relates the spinning ride to life. She says things like, "If you think about negatives, stop it, and remember, 'I believe in myself; I like me.' Don't let people rent space in your head; stay away from negative energy. Create positive energy and share it with others. Give it away! Believe in yourself. Life has hills just like this spin class, and how you take it on shows your strength to get through anything. Sometimes it's good to get out of your comfort zone and see what you're really made of."

She also takes people to their feel-good zone throughout the ride, asking students to think of something that makes them smile and to really focus on it. Her motive going into each class is to give her students 100 percent of herself, and her goal is that they walk away from the class more positive than when they arrived. She explains that sometimes there is a little hurt, but with a few more pushes and a little more endurance, you can make it through anything and come out stronger, just like in life.

B uses fitness analogies in most things she does. She likened her pregnancy to doing a half Ironman competition. The first trimester was a 1.2-mile swim in open waters: not too hard, but uncomfortable with some nervous, anxious feelings. The second trimester was a 56-mile bike ride: most of the time she was on cloud nine, feeling confident and great (this is her favorite activity). The third trimester was a half-marathon run. She says she was saying to herself, "This is getting hard, but I am almost there, and I can feel the sense of victory and accomplishment, and I can see the finish line."

B has now been teaching for more than twenty years and still gets just as excited before each class as she did when she was seventeen. B's spirit, caring, and customer service have excelled her in her career and has helped make her fitness studio one that people cannot wait to go to.

NOTES

1. **Face your demons head-on daily.** We all have fears or insecurities. Know what they are, and face them with a can-do attitude and a positive outlook. It has been said by successful people that if one person can do it, so can others.

2. **Use your strengths to their fullest and see how you can inspire others.** When people see true strength in others, it is quite natural for them to be inspired. It is human nature to love to see someone try.

3. **Follow your dreams.** If you love something that you do, do it to the best of your ability. Throw yourself into it fully and take it as far as you can. It may bring you great success and, if it doesn't, something else will show up for you, and try that.

4. **Take lessons from the people in your life—even the little people.** Stay in tune with how others affect you emotionally, mentally, and physically. Observe, learn, and pass it on. B did just this. Fitness really helped her get back into shape after her baby was born, and being surrounded by positive energy at her studio made all the difference in the world.

5. **Self-talk really works.** Just like we really are what we eat, we really are and can become what we tell ourselves we are. What you think about yourself, you bring about.

WorkIT!

Write down what your biggest strength or strengths are, use them, and focus your actions on them every single day and in all you do. Utilize these strengths, especially when dealing with your customers. They will notice and react positively. Human nature is to celebrate others, to see them successful and want to be like them. It is *not* human nature to be jealous of the positive traits in others.

_____

_____

_____

_____

_____

Focus your career path on a job that utilizes your strengths. Write them down on paper for clarity, and look at your list daily. Add new strengths as you recognize them or further develop more strengths.

_____

_____

_____

_____

_____

_____

If you have always had a dream to do something in your life, make a short-term and long-term plan on paper to map out how you can get there. Every day and in everything you do, work toward this goal.

_____

_____

_____

_____

_____

_____

Write down one thing you are afraid of, and work on facing that fear every day. You will eventually become comfortable with it and learn to overcome it. Then move on to another fear you have and do the same. Keep going. Use these newfound assets when dealing with others in your life, especially at work.

_____

_____

_____

_____

_____

_____

_____

Think about who inspires you, even if it is in a small way. Write this down. Think about how you can apply what you learned from this inspiration to your daily life. Write these down on paper and read them daily—one step at a time, one action at a time, and then do it.

_____

_____

_____

_____

_____

_____

_____

CHAPTER 12

CUSTOMER SERVICE THOUGHTS

WE feel fortunate to have had the experience of interviewing all the amazing people who are featured in this book. We have learned so much and have been inspired by their examples. As we interviewed, we had lots of questions we continued to ask ourselves, consumed with curiosity as to *what makes a successful person tick*. And as we let others know we were writing this book, they had questions as well. Here are the some of the questions that have been rattling around in our minds throughout this entire process.

Are people born with a "customer service gene" or do they just develop it along the way?

Okay, this is a fascinating question. Is it nature or nurture? It's an age-old question. We believe that there are people who certainly are born with some personal characteristics that make them more *likely* to be motivated, have momentum, and to be great at serving customers. However, we also noted in many of our interviews that even if you were born with those qualities, life (which seems to be a stand-up comedian) often has a funny way of testing your level of commitment. Many of our interview subjects were faced with tremendous and painful amounts of soul-crushing adversity. But despite that adversity—yes, you guessed it—remained motivated.

Are people who have a customer service mindset in any sort of particular income, geographic, ethnic, or gender group?

The answer is without a doubt no. No. No. No. No. Okay, enough nos. The people we interviewed who have these special qualities are not restricted to a particular label of gender, race, creed, color, ethnicity, or religion. In fact, it almost seems to be the opposite of that idea. People with these special qualities seem to transcend the label that the world at large wishes to apply to them. It's almost as if to them it does not matter. They refuse to be labeled and do not allow any label to hold them back. We saw people with a great service attitude who were only sixteen years old and people who were senior citizens. Age to them seemed not to matter. In fact, in most cases they chose to ignore it (maybe a lesson for all of us). Age is only a number! This is where the mental aspect comes into play.

Do people who have a great service mindset know that they have it?

That is also an interesting question. We found many of the people we interviewed possessed a humble attitude and were very interested in serving others. They were confident but not arrogant, not bashful but also not boastful. If you ask each one of them if they were motivated, our guess is that they probably would say, "I'm not sure if I am motivated, but I am an optimistic person." What we do know is that other people who meet someone who has this quality can automatically tell they have it. They have a spark, energy, and enthusiasm about them; a passion for life and for people; and as we describe in many cases, they are like a magnet that draws other people to them. It's kind of like the definition of great art, it's hard to describe but you know it is great when you see it. These special people contained within the pages of this book are people magnets. They inspire and motivate others. They are great at service.

Can someone learn to develop his or her level of customer service commitment?

Of course! If we did not believe that people could develop the skill sets, then there would be no point in writing this book. The entire point of this book is to acknowledge that people do have the power and the ability to change their mindset and to change their life and their customers' lives. We encourage you to go back to each chapter and read the key points and the Notes at the end to figure out how you can apply them to your work.

We believe that your life—what you have, what you do, and how you feel about it—is entirely up to you. You are the architect of your own life. So build it. Humans are the only species that we know of who have the ability to change their lives through the act of conscious thought. We have never seen a turtle sitting on a log with a planner in his hand. Everyone we interviewed reinforced these exact concepts over and over again.

Why does having a great customer service attitude matter?

Well, it is actually quite simple. People are attracted to people who have motivation, momentum, and a great attitude. If you do not believe this to be true, here are a few questions to ask yourself: If you were an employer, would you want to hire an employee who had these qualities or one who did not? Hello? If you were dating, would you want to date someone who had these qualities or not? If you were trying to find someone to be your best friend, would you want somebody who had these qualities or did not have them? How about who to talk to at a party? How about your doctor or a dentist? In the seat next to you on the plane ride to Buffalo? Your cube mate at work? Invariably, answers to all of these questions would be a resounding yes! Since this is all true, then *you* want to be someone who has a great customer service attitude, and you want to be with people who have it.

Isn't the concept of everyone having great customer service skills unrealistic?

Yes. No. Maybe. But as for us, we will continue to be unrealistic, over-optimistic dreamers. We plead guilty and throw ourselves at the mercy of the world court! The reality is that we don't care about the verdict. Being folks with the right attitude ourselves, we believe that everybody has the capability to live up to their full potential. We also believe that everyone can develop increased levels of motivation, momentum, and a service mindset. Will everyone have it? No, because some people will reject the concept entirely and will continue to be cynical, negative naysayers. That is their choice; it is called freedom of choice (that is why it's called freedom) or free will. People can decide to be unmotivated, have no momentum, and have a lousy attitude toward service. They also have the choice to be miserable and depressed. That *is* a choice.

One of the key elements that we found from the people we interviewed was that every one of them just flat-out *decided* to choose to reinvent their life and to be motivated, refusing to listen to the cynical, negative people in the world. So if everyone having the right mindset is unrealistic, that is okay with us. We still choose this. We take what is behind door #3. There will always be some people who are too shortsighted or stubborn to change and are satisfied with living a life with limitations. Too sad. It will be their limited life.

In our interviews we were delighted with the variety of people, personalities, and occupations we got to know. We also wondered if there was some sort of commonality among the entire group that we could lay down to say, "Here is what these folks have in common." Was there a thread? We have been able to identify fifteen traits:

1. They want to be the best.

Everyone we talked to had an overwhelming desire and an internal drive to be the best at what they do, but also to be the best person they could be. It did not matter whether they ran a fitness studio, were a skycap, or a professional speaker, they had a commitment to being the best and took real pride in their work. Just because. They didn't always need a reason. You could assume that they developed that attitude from the people who raised them, but as you have already read, there are many exceptions to prove that this is not true. Many of the folks we interviewed had developed the attitude on their own, despite the fact that they were in either abusive or negative situations. You might describe them as self-made, which gives hope to all of us.

2. They have a positive attitude.

No matter what happens they look at life through a lens that is colored for happiness. The glass is half full. They truly look on the bright side of life. Many folks we spoke to surprised us by saying that they decided to be happy no matter what happened to them, and even despite what happened to some of them. It was kind of a stubborn form of happiness. Every day when these folks get up, they decide to be happy. Even though they may be in jobs where they're required to serve hot dogs, process fish, or handle luggage, they still get up every day with a positive attitude, actually looking forward to their work, not dreading it. Their glass is always more than half full, and they don't understand people who see the glass as half empty. They make lemonade out of oranges.

3. They have faced adversity.

The people we interviewed have faced every range of adversity from racism to physical and mental abuse to being poor to nearly dying of circumstances that were either of their own doing or a life circumstance. The key with every one of these people is no matter what the adversity was, they got right back up again and just kept on going. They're like the old-fashioned inflatable children's punch toy that was weighted on the bottom. You punch it and it just gets back up. Many people reminded us of the song by the band Chumbawamba titled "I Get Knocked Down." In the chorus they sing gleefully, "I get knocked down, but I get up again, you're never gonna keep me down." These folks don't believe in giving up. Not an option! Adversity will not win in their lives.

4. *They embrace opportunity.*

Every single person we talked to embraced opportunity when it came to him or her, whether it was difficult or not. They had the uncanny ability to identify a short-term opportunity that would lead to long-term success. They trusted their guts. They also embraced opportunity even when they faced fearful situations or a situation where they've never done the thing before. To them, that really didn't matter if it was new— they just kept plowing forward knowing that things would work out...and they did. Many of them also stated that they were willing to change their occupation multiple times and would try one type of work, try another, and then try another yet again until they found the right fit for their talents. How many people say, "I'm afraid to leave the job that I have because I might not like the next one?" Nope, not these fine people. That was never an issue for any of these folks. Their philosophy was, "If I have an opportunity, I'm going to take advantage of it."

5. They love hard work.

Every person we interviewed always had the amazing quality of having the work ethic of a Morgan plow horse. They work hard, have worked hard, and continue to work hard. They know the value of hard work and really don't mind doing it. Their work may have been hard physically or mentally, or they had more than one job at the same time. They never complained about it or whined about it or even made it sound like it was a negative; they just did what they did, and they kept doing it. They loved it. Additionally, many of these people were not only working hard but were also busy with other life activities—completing degrees and other training while they were working. People like this think that laziness is a foreign concept and don't understand it. Laziness is just not in their DNA. They think it is crazy to be lazy.

6. They are persistent.

Every person in this book has the amazing quality of endless dogged persistence. They would ride a bicycle 31 miles, put up with abuse, work for many hours with low pay, work at places that were run in ways they did not enjoy, but they were always persistent and always had an idea of what they were going to do in the future. Many times when asked, they would say things like, "I don't give up," or "I don't quit," or "there is no quit in me." Many people just simply don't view quitting as a viable option. This is a very admirable quality and one that some people in the world don't have, often giving up right before they have reached a level of success.

7. *They tap into resources.*

They don't leave things to chance; they look around to find resources that are available to them. It might be a book, a church, a mentor, or a training program, but these people do not sit around on their hands waiting for something. Not a chance. They find the resource and tap into it. We also found that as part of that process, they were willing to ask other people where the resources were located and how to find them. They realized that someone out there knows what they need to know and they realize that someone has also been successful at it before them. They are not necessarily wise but they are seeking wisdom from those who possess it. They know where to find it, and if they don't, they just keep looking until they do. They ask, question, investigate, research, and keep at it.

8. *They don't limit their thinking.*

They are not tied to a limited belief system that says they can't do what they want to do. Their position, background, and economic status are irrelevant. Why can't they be a millionaire? Why can't they start a business from scratch and have it be successful? Why can't they change the world around them and have an impact? Why can't they move to a foreign country? Why can't they start a revolution? They are not defined by position or place or title. People telling them what they can't do does not discourage them. In fact, it does the opposite. They use it as a motivator to prove to other people that their thinking and judgment was flawed. They refuse to think in a small way; they only think about the massive possibilities, and know that it starts with their thinking first. These people are big thinkers. They set goals some others would think are crazy and unrealistic. They are really not too concerned with the limited opinions of others.

9. They are learners.

All of the people we interviewed are not just learners, but many of them are what we call "super learners." They have an innate sense of curiosity about how things work. They have gone to school, attended training programs, enrolled in colleges, received certifications, and read tons of books. They all understand that in order to be successful they need to keep learning and keep growing. They do not believe in stagnation, only motivation. They are always trying to figure out how they can learn and where they can learn it. When it comes to learning, for them it is a lifelong process that will continue until the day they die. They want the know-how, and they want it now.

10. They are unique.

People in this book don't seem to be very interested in fitting in with the crowd or being like everyone else. They are proud to be unique and different, and they don't mind other people thinking of them as unique, special, or even at times eccentric. The pressures of society do not tremendously sway them and what other people think; they are more interested in doing what it takes to accomplish their goals. Ironically, the fact that they are unique and not so interested in conforming to the social norms causes them to be admired for this quality by others who don't have the courage to be different. That is, of course, the ultimate irony. The very society that gives them a hard time for being different admires them for being that way.

11. They embrace life.

To a person, everyone we interviewed took life by the horns and wrestled it to the ground. They embrace life with a spirit of vim and vigor. They realize that life is short, and they're going to make sure they treat every day with the value it deserves. They are people who accomplish things, get things done, and are the "doers" of our world. At the same time, they also enjoy life overall, embracing their experiences and their passions. They are the kind of people who do not want to retire at the end of their life and look back on a life consumed by the disease of regret. They will make mistakes but they will go for it and no one will ever accuse them of not embracing life to the fullest.

12. They are brave.

They have the courage of determination and a spirit of getting it done, allowing them to have courage even when they're scared. This "give it a try" attitude allows them to often try things that other people would not even consider doing. They face their demons. After all, starting your own business is risky, fraught with difficulties, and leads to some anxious moments. The folks that we interviewed, however, have always felt that the risk in the end will always be outweighed by the rewards. If you're not willing to take the risk, then you would not be able to gain the rewards. They're willing to take a shot.

13. They have heroes and mentors.

During the many conversations we had, the person we were talking to mentioned some hero or mentor whom they had been exposed to and had learned a great deal from. It may have been a parent, a teacher, a business partner, a friend, or even a person in a book, but they found people in their lives who were willing to help them, guide them, direct them, and support them. These mentors and masters obviously had a tremendous impact on these folks, and these people were always willing to give that person/mentor complete and full credit for what they had done for them. We suspect that most successful people in life have been shaped by their mentors and heroes, and those who are not as successful are not because they have not sought out mentors and advisors in their life.

14. They are willing to give up the hunt.

Everyone in life has failures, either in their personal life or in their professional life. Probably both. The folks we talked to were very persistent; however, they also had the common sense to know when it was time to give something up and move on to some other endeavor. Let's face it, sometimes the rocket does not leave the pad; sometimes you fail a test or lose a friend. Sometimes the homecoming queen *does not* go out with you and goes out with someone else (darn). These people were willing to face the failure when it did not work and simply moved on to something else without letting this failure define their future in a negative way.

15. They follow their instincts.

Many times when we asked why someone did something or took some sort of action, they said they just had a gut instinct or felt it was the right thing to do. They would even say, "I don't know...I just had a feeling." The difference with these people is that they were willing to listen to their instincts, and they were willing to trust their gut and to take action accordingly because they trust themselves.

Are these subjects featured in our book all perfect? Of course not. They are human beings who have quirks and frailties like anyone else. We are all flawed in this lifetime. However, these folks do possess special qualities we can all learn from if we are willing to open our eyes our ears and our hearts.

They volunteered willingly to share their stories in the hopes that their stories would help you, our reader, improve your customer service life. We felt a particular vital responsibility to tell each of these stories about these special, wonderful people and to do them justice. Telling someone else's story is always something we feel a little more obligation about—to write about *his or her* truth.

But here is what we have learned and that we would like to leave you with, in closing: We thank you for spending time with us and we beg you to embrace this content and apply it to *your* world.

If in reading this you have determined that you are not happy with your current level of customer service or just part of your life, then change it. You have the ability to change it, as you are after all the architect of your own existence. We have both seen in our careers as speakers and trainers tremendous success stories, people who changed because they decided to. It is our heartfelt hope that we can have an impact on your life by sharing these stories as well. There is always another in life that anyone of us can learn from. There will always be someone who knows something we do not. You can continue to learn. You can continue to reinvent yourself.

Last, we want you to realize from reading these stories that anything is truly possible. We believe many of the people in this book will achieve the next level of their big dreams. Anything *is* truly possible, and history has certainly taught us that. Remember that people were sent to the moon only as a result of a group of human beings who thought it was possible. Many people said it was a ridiculous and a fruitless effort and it would never happen. History proved them wrong.

So here is the truly big question: Are you going to allow your past to determine your future; to allow cynical people of the world to define your path? We hope not. We hope this book and the amazing stories of these people will help convince you that you can give great customer service with rewards beyond your wildest dreams.

Now

go

give

GREAT SERVICE!

ABOUT THE AUTHORS

Shawn Doyle CSP is a learning and development professional who has a passion for human potential. He has an avid belief in the concept of life-long learning. For the last 22 years, Shawn has spent his time developing and implementing training programs on team building, communication, creativity and leadership. Shawn's training programs help people become more effective in the workplace and in their lives. His clients have included numerous Fortune 500 companies, and his awards and honors are extensive. Shawn is the author of ten inspirational books.

Lauren Anderson is highly sought after as a Consultant, Mentor and Spokesperson. Her company focuses on Training People Development in the retail luxury goods arena. She is a frequent and recognizable guest on national television and writes numerous articles for top specialty and professional publications.